GEORGIA O'KEEFFE

Paul Strand: *Georgia O'Keeffe*. Copyright © 1979, Aperture Foundation Inc., Paul Strand Archive.

AMERICAN WOMEN of ACHIEVEMENT

GEORGIA O'KEEFFE

MICHAEL BERRY

CHELSEA HOUSE PUBLISHERS

NEW YORK • PHILADELPHIA

Chelsea House Publishers
EDITOR-IN-CHIEF: Nancy Toff
EXECUTIVE EDITOR: Remmel T. Nunn
MANAGING EDITOR: Karyn Gullen Browne
COPY CHIEF: Juliann Barbato
PICTURE EDITOR: Adrian G. Allen
ART DIRECTOR: Giannella Garrett
MANUFACTURING MANAGER: Gerald Levine

American Women of Achievement
SENIOR EDITOR: Constance Jones

Staff for GEORGIA O'KEEFFE
ASSISTANT EDITOR: Maria Behan
COPY EDITOR: Karen Hammonds
DEPUTY COPY CHIEF: Ellen Scordato
EDITORIAL ASSISTANT: Theodore Keyes
PICTURE RESEARCHER: Linda Peer
DESIGN: Design Oasis
ASSISTANT DESIGNER: Donna Sinisgalli
PRODUCTION COORDINATOR: Joseph Romano
COVER ILLUSTRATOR: Susan Barrasi

Library of Congress Cataloging in Publication Data

Berry, Michael L.
Georgia O'Keeffe.

(American women of achievement)
Bibliography: p.
Includes index.

Summary: A biography of the noted American artist who found
much of her artistic inspiration in nature, especially the desert
landscape of the Southwest.
1. O'Keeffe, Georgia, 1887–1986—Juvenile literature.   2. Artists—
United States—Biography—Juvenile literature.   [1. O'Keeffe, Georgia, 1887–1986.   2. Artists.]   I. Title.   II. Series.

N6537.039B47   1988   759.13   [B]   [92]   87-23928

ISBN 1-55546-673-7
        0-7910-0420-1 (pbk.)

CONTENTS

AMERICAN WOMEN of ACHIEVEMENT

Abigail Adams
women's rights advocate

Jane Addams
social worker

Louisa May Alcott
author

Marian Anderson
singer

Susan B. Anthony
woman suffragist

Ethel Barrymore
actress

Clara Barton
founder of the American Red Cross

Elizabeth Blackwell
physician

Nellie Bly
journalist

Margaret Bourke-White
photographer

Pearl Buck
author

Rachel Carson
biologist and author

Mary Cassatt
artist

Agnes De Mille
choreographer

Emily Dickinson
poet

Isadora Duncan
dancer

Amelia Earhart
aviator

Mary Baker Eddy
founder of the Christian Science church

Betty Friedan
feminist

Althea Gibson
tennis champion

Emma Goldman
political activist

Helen Hayes
actress

Lillian Hellman
playwright

Katharine Hepburn
actress

Karen Horney
psychoanalyst

Anne Hutchinson
religious leader

Mahalia Jackson
gospel singer

Helen Keller
humanitarian

Jeane Kirkpatrick
diplomat

Emma Lazarus
poet

Clare Boothe Luce
author and diplomat

Barbara McClintock
biologist

Margaret Mead
anthropologist

Edna St. Vincent Millay
poet

Julia Morgan
architect

Grandma Moses
painter

Louise Nevelson
sculptor

Sandra Day O'Connor
Supreme Court justice

Georgia O'Keeffe
painter

Eleanor Roosevelt
diplomat and humanitarian

Wilma Rudolph
champion athlete

Florence Sabin
medical researcher

Beverly Sills
opera singer

Gertrude Stein
author

Gloria Steinem
feminist

Harriet Beecher Stowe
author and abolitionist

Mae West
entertainer

Edith Wharton
author

Phillis Wheatley
poet

Babe Didrikson Zaharias
champion athlete

CHELSEA HOUSE PUBLISHERS

"Remember the Ladies"

MATINA S. HORNER

Remember the Ladies." That is what Abigail Adams wrote to her husband John, then a delegate to the Continental Congress, as the Founding Fathers met in Philadelphia to form a new nation in March of 1776. "Be more generous and favorable to them than your ancestors. Do not put such unlimited power in the hands of the Husbands. If particular care and attention is not paid to the Ladies," Abigail Adams warned, "we are determined to foment a Rebellion, and will not hold ourselves bound by any Laws in which we have no voice, or Representation."

The words of Abigail Adams, one of the earliest American advocates of women's rights, were prophetic. Because when we have not "remembered the ladies," they have, by their words and deeds, reminded us so forcefully of the omission that we cannot fail to remember them. For the history of American women is as interesting and varied as the history of our nation as a whole. American women have played an integral part in founding, settling, and building our country. Some we remember as remarkable women who—against great odds—achieved distinction in the public arena: Anne Hutchinson, who in the 17th century became a charismatic religious leader; Phillis Wheatley, an 18th-century black slave who became a poet; Susan B. Anthony, whose name is synonymous with the 19th-century women's rights movement, and who led the struggle to enfranchise women; and, in our own century, Amelia Earhart, the first woman to cross the Atlantic Ocean by air.

These extraordinary women certainly merit our admiration, but other women, "common women," many of them all but forgotten, should also be recognized for their contributions to American thought and culture. Women have been community builders; they have founded schools and formed voluntary associations to help those in need; they have assumed the major responsibility for rearing children, passing on from one generation to the next the values that keep a culture alive. These and innumerable other contributions, once ignored, are now being recognized by scholars, students, and the public. It is exciting and gratifying to realize that a part of our history that was hardly acknowledged a few generations ago is now being studied and brought to light.

In recent decades, the field of women's history has grown from obscurity to a politically controversial splinter movement to academic respectability, in many cases mainstreamed into such traditional disciplines as history, economics, and psychology. Scholars of women, both female and male, have organized research centers at such prestigious institutions as Wellesley College, Stanford University, and the University of California. Other notable centers for women's studies are the Center for the American Woman and Politics at the Eagleton Institute of Politics at Rutgers University; the Henry A. Murray Research Center for the Study of Lives, at Radcliffe College; and the Women's Research and Education Institute, the research arm of the Congressional Caucus on Women's Issues. Other scholars and public figures have established archives and libraries, such as the Schlesinger Library on the History of Women in America, at Radcliffe College, and the Sophia Smith Collection, at Smith College, to collect and preserve the written and tangible legacies of women.

From the initial donation of the Women's Rights Collection in 1943, the Schlesinger Library grew to encompass vast collections documenting the manifold accomplishments of American women. Simultaneously, the women's movement in general and the academic discipline of women's studies in particular also began with a narrow definition and gradually expanded their mandate. Early causes such as woman suffrage and social reform, abolition and organized labor were joined by newer concerns such as the history of women in business and the professions and in politics and government; the study of the family; and social issues such as health policy and education.

Women, as historian Arthur M. Schlesinger, jr., once pointed out, "have constituted the most spectacular casualty of traditional history. They have made up at least half the human race, but you could never tell that by looking at the books historians write." The new breed of historians is remedying that omission. They have written books about immigrant women and about working-class women who struggled for survival in cities and about black women who met the challenges of life in rural areas. They are telling the stories of women who, despite the barriers of tradition and economics, became lawyers and doctors and public figures.

The women's studies movement has also led scholars to question traditional interpretations of their respective disciplines. For example, the study of war has traditionally been an exercise in military and political analysis, an examination of strategies planned and executed by men. But scholars of women's history have pointed out that wars have also been periods of tremendous change and even opportunity for women, because the very absence of men on the home front enabled them to expand their educational, economic, and professional activities and to assume leadership in their homes.

The early scholars of women's history showed a unique brand of courage in choosing to investigate new subjects and take new approaches to old ones. Often, like their subjects, they endured criticism and even ostracism by their academic colleagues. But their efforts have unquestionably been worthwhile, because with the publication of each new study and book another piece of the historical patchwork is sewn into place, revealing an increasingly comprehensive picture of the role of women in our rich and varied history.

Such books on groups of women are essential, but books that focus on the lives of individuals are equally indispensable. Biographies can be inspirational, offering their readers the example of people with vision who have looked outside themselves for their goals and have often struggled against great obstacles to achieve them. Marian Anderson, for instance, had to overcome racial bigotry in order to perfect her art and perform as a concert singer. Isadora Duncan defied the rules of classical dance to find true artistic freedom. Jane Addams had to break down society's notions of the proper role for women in order to create new social institutions, notably the settlement house. All of these women had to come to terms both with themselves and with the world in which they lived. Only then could they move ahead as pioneers in their chosen callings.

Biography can inspire not only by adulation but also by realism. It helps us to see not only the qualities in others that we hope to emulate, but also, perhaps, the weaknesses that made them "human." By helping us identify with the subject on a more personal level they help us to feel that we, too, can achieve such goals. We read about Eleanor Roosevelt, for instance, who occupied a unique and seemingly enviable position as the wife of the president. Yet we can sympathize with her inner dilemma: an inherently shy woman, she had to force herself to live a most public life in order to use her position to benefit others. We may not be able to imagine ourselves having the immense poetic talent of Emily Dickinson, but from her story we can understand the challenges faced by a creative woman who was expected to fulfill many family responsibilities. And though few of us will ever reach the level of athletic accomplishment displayed by Wilma Rudolph or Babe Zaharias, we can still appreciate their spirit, their overwhelming will to excel.

A biography is a multifaceted lens. It is first of all a magnification, the intimate examination of one particular life. But at the same time, it is a wide-angle lens, informing us about the world in which the subject lived. We come away from reading about one life knowing more about the social, political, and economic fabric of the time. It is for this reason, perhaps, that the great New England essayist Ralph Waldo Emerson wrote, in 1841, "There is properly no history: only biography." And it is also why biography, and particularly women's biography, will continue to fascinate writers and readers alike.

GEORGIA O'KEEFFE

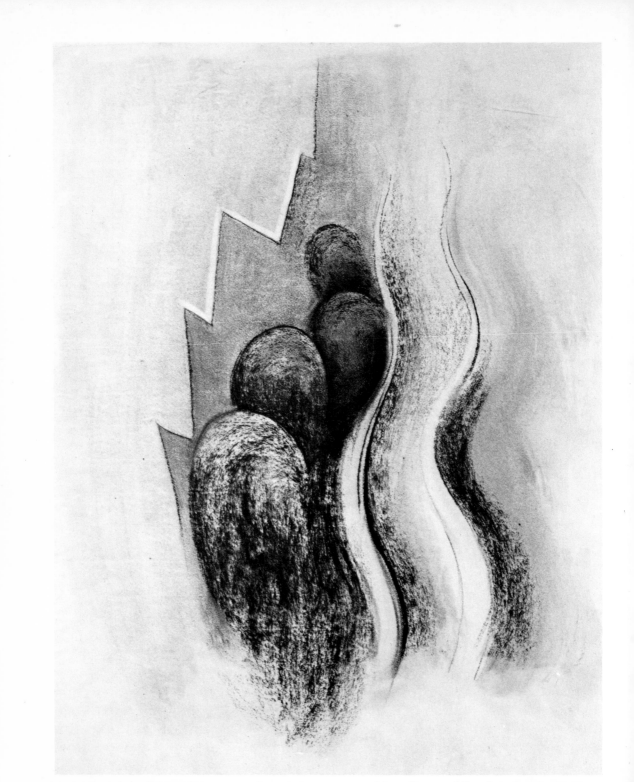

Georgia O'Keeffe's striking Drawing XIII was part of her first public showing in 1916. Alfred Stieglitz mounted the exhibition at his 291 Gallery without the artist's permission.

ONE

Debut at "291"

It was 1916, and 28-year-old Georgia O'Keeffe was furious with photographer and gallery owner Alfred Stieglitz. His prestigious gallery at 291 Fifth Avenue in New York City, usually referred to simply as "291," regularly displayed some of Europe's and America's most exciting modern art. O'Keeffe, a painter and art teacher, admired Stieglitz greatly but decided that he still had no right to do what he had done to her. She was determined to have it out with him.

While eating in the cafeteria at Columbia University Teachers College earlier that day, she had been approached by a woman who asked whether she was "Virginia O'Keeffe." When O'Keeffe said that she was not, the woman explained that drawings by someone of that name were on display at Stieglitz's 291.

O'Keeffe realized that the drawings were her own. Without her permission—without even using her correct name—Stieglitz had put her deeply personal drawings on display for crowds of strangers to see. As O'Keeffe later wrote in her autobiography, "For me the drawings were private and the idea of their being hung on the wall for the public to look at was just too much."

She immediately set off for Stieglitz's gallery, which was housed in an unpretentious brownstone located at Fifth Avenue and Thirty-first Street. When she arrived at 291, O'Keeffe discovered that Stieglitz was away on jury duty. The tongue-lashing would have to be postponed, but she decided to have a look around anyway. Despite her anger, O'Keeffe noticed that her drawings occupied the gallery's largest

Stieglitz took this photograph of O'Keeffe in 1918 at his family's home in Lake George, New York. Although their friendship got off to a rocky start, the two artists soon embarked on a 30-year relationship.

room. The work of two male artists was relegated to smaller areas. Stieglitz had clearly taken great care in mounting her drawings, which were displayed in the best possible light: natural sunlight that flooded through a skylight. A burnished brass vase filled with colorful dried flowers had been placed on a platform at the center of the room.

O'Keeffe had first encountered Stieg-litz in 1907, while studying at the Art Students League in New York. A native of Hoboken, New Jersey, Stieglitz was one of the earliest champions of photography as a serious art form. Among his many other technical and artistic accomplishments, Stieglitz was the first photographer to take successful pictures at night and during storms.

At that first meeting, O'Keeffe had

Alfred Stieglitz's experiments with photography advanced the medium as an art form. Winter 5th Avenue *(1892) captures New York City in a snowstorm.*

Der Raucher (The Smoker) *is one of the vibrant creations of painter Paul Cézanne. Stieglitz's 291 introduced many Americans to Cézanne and other ground-breaking European artists.*

larger room at the back, that Americans first saw the paintings of such modern European masters as Pablo Picasso and Paul Cézanne. One day O'Keeffe hoped to join the ranks of innovative artists that Stieglitz had discovered. In a letter to friend and fellow artist, Anita Pollitzer, she confided, "I believe I would rather have Stieglitz like something—anything I have done—than anyone else I know of."

Early that year, O'Keeffe had been teaching in South Carolina when she sent several new drawings to Pollitzer in New York. She wanted Pollitzer's opinion on the abstract charcoal sketches. They represented a departure from O'Keeffe's earlier work, in which she painstakingly reproduced objects and landscapes on canvas and paper. Her friend was immediately impressed. "I was struck by their aliveness," Pollitzer later remarked. "They were different. Here were charcoals— on the same kind of paper that all art students were using, and through no trick, no superiority of tools, these drawings were saying something that had not yet been said."

Soon after she received them, Pollitzer stood outside 291 with O'Keeffe's drawings in hand. She knew that O'Keeffe was reluctant to show her drawings to people she did not know well, but she also knew how much her friend admired Stieglitz. She went in and found him alone in his attic, weary from a long day. The middle-aged pho-

been intimidated by the outspoken photographer and had said almost nothing to him. Now, 11 years later, she still kept her distance from the flamboyant art patron, although she often visited his gallery to view the works on display. The artists shown by Stieglitz infused their work with an emotional intensity and a sense of bold experimentation that O'Keeffe greatly admired. It was in this crowded gallery, consisting of little more than a small front room, a hallway, and a

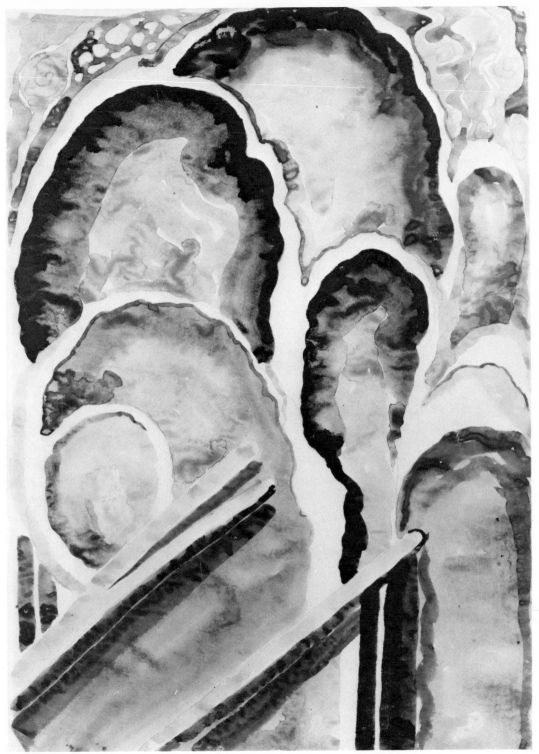

Blue #1, a 1916 watercolor, is one of O'Keeffe's first abstract paintings. Although her earliest, traditional work showed great promise, her remarkable personal style emerged only after she began experimenting with abstract forms.

tographer, always eager to look at new work, inspected O'Keeffe's drawings in silence. Then he looked up, smiled, and, according to later reports, declared, "At last, a woman on paper!" He went on to call the drawings the "purest, finest, sincerest things that have entered 291 in a long while," and he casually mentioned that he might want to display them sometime.

Pollitzer quickly wrote to O'Keeffe, confessing what she had done. O'Keeffe was not angry. Pollitzer had correctly guessed that O'Keeffe had wanted her to take the drawings to Stieglitz all along but did not dare face him—and any possible criticisms—herself.

Although O'Keeffe valued Stieglitz's opinion of her art, she was still indignant when she moved back to New York and discovered that he had hung her drawings without asking her permission. A week after she first went to upbraid him, O'Keeffe once again rode the rickety, hand-pulled elevator to the attic of 291. This time, Stieglitz was in the gallery. O'Keeffe's anger made her fearless; she walked right up to him and insisted that he take down her drawings at once. A bushy-haired man with a bristling white mustache, Stieglitz stared at the slender, dark-haired young woman addressing him. She was dramatically dressed all in black, except for the simple white collar around her throat. Stieglitz refused to take down her drawings. "He said he wanted them on the wall to look at,"

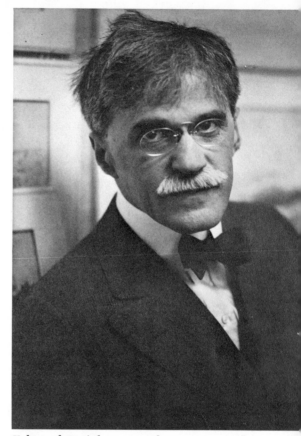

Edward Steichen, another renowned photographer, took this portrait of Stieglitz at 291.

O'Keeffe later reported in her autobiography.

Stieglitz kept talking, praising O'Keeffe's drawings, and finally she softened. He may have exhibited her work without her knowledge, and his attitude might have been patronizing, but he certainly understood and respected her art. When Stieglitz finally ran out of steam, O'Keeffe gave in and asked what he planned to do with the drawings once the show was over. He promised to take exceptional care of them and return them at once. He also asked to see more of her work. A strong woman used to getting her own way, O'Keeffe must have left 291 wondering how he had changed her mind so easily.

At the beginning of the 20th century, most members of the art establishment did not take women seriously as artists. Stieglitz, however, was a rare exception. He believed that the female experience of life was fundamentally different from that of the male. He felt that these differences left women freer of crippling societal inhibitions and enabled female artists to express vividly personal visions. In his eyes, the bold lines and shapes of O'Keeffe's abstract drawings were unmistakably the work of such an intensely expressive woman. At the time she was creating them, O'Keeffe had written to Pollitzer, "The thing seems to express in a way what I wanted it to but—it also seems rather effeminate—it is essentially a woman's feeling—[it] satisfies me in a way."

As Stieglitz had foreseen, the drawings caused a stir. Critics, artists, and other spectators filled the gallery, anxious to see these drawings by an unknown female art teacher. Many were shocked by what they found.

What scandalized some was the erotic energy of the drawings. Although they were abstract, the drawings managed to convey a powerful sensuality. Disturbed by their frankness, art critic Willard H. Wright complained to Stieglitz, "All these pictures say is 'I want to have a baby.' " Stieglitz was unruffled. "That's fine," he replied, "a woman has painted a picture telling you that she wants to have a baby." Stieglitz saw nothing wrong with art that expressed sexual feeling. He believed that America needed to free itself of its repressive attitude and allow artists full creative freedom.

Reveling in the controversy he helped cause, Stieglitz extended the show into July. By then, O'Keeffe had left New York to teach summer school at the University of Virginia. But she left with a sense of triumph. After years of study, her unorthodox and highly original drawings had at last been displayed in public, and they had certainly created a sensation.

O'Keeffe's debut at 291 was a turning point in her life. It marked the beginning of her association with Alfred Stieglitz, the genius who would become her mentor and eventually her husband. Relying on his and her own confidence in her artistic gifts, she would go on to build a reputation as one of America's greatest painters.

An art teacher lectures her pupils in a typical early 20th-century classroom. Although she disliked the formal environment of her school in Sun Prairie, Wisconsin, Georgia was a good student who particularly enjoyed art class.

TWO

Sun Prairie and Williamsburg

The prairies of the American Midwest were the first landscapes to capture the imagination of Georgia Totto O'Keeffe. Born on November 15, 1887, to Francis and Ida O'Keeffe, she spent the first 14 years of her life in Sun Prairie, Wisconsin, a quiet farm community 12 miles outside Madison, the state capital.

Georgia was the second child and first daughter in the O'Keeffe household. First-born Francis, Jr., was a year and a half older. Georgia was followed by five younger siblings, four sisters and a brother.

Although she had six brothers and sisters, Georgia usually preferred to play by herself, away from her siblings and the scrutiny of the adults. When the weather was good, she could often be found sitting beneath the apple trees on her front lawn, quietly playing with a set of china dolls. From the very beginning, O'Keeffe was adept at entertaining herself. As she remarked in later years, "I've never been bored."

One of Georgia's first drawings was a pencil sketch of a man bending over. She labored over the picture for quite a while but could not make the man's legs bend correctly at both the hips and the knees. When she turned the paper upside down, however, she found that he looked fine—as a man lying on his back with his legs extended straight up into the air. In her autobiography, O'Keeffe recalled, "I thought it a very funny position for a man, but after all my effort it gave me a feeling of real achievement to have made something—even if it wasn't what I had intended."

A giant snake threatens to devour a man in this illustration from The Arabian Nights, *one of the adventure stories that mesmerized the young O'Keeffe.*

Although a very independent child, Georgia did not lack for love and affection. Both of her grandmothers lived nearby, as did a number of aunts and uncles, many of whom took an interest in young Georgia. Her father, the son of Irish immigrants who had settled in Wisconsin to farm, was a good-natured, gentle man. Georgia's mother, the daughter of a Hungarian count who had fled political turmoil in his homeland, was a serious, intelligent woman who had once dreamed of becoming a doctor. When she married Frank O'Keeffe and started a family, she focused on developing her children's confidence and intellectual curiosity. As O'Keeffe later told her younger sister, "Our mother had a very good opinion of herself, and she

wanted all of us to be the same way."

Busy with the physical challenges of raising a frontier family, Ida O'Keeffe nevertheless found time to encourage a love of learning in her children, the girls as well as the boys. She especially loved reading aloud to her children in the evenings. Because Georgia's older brother, Francis, Jr., usually chose the story their mother would read, Georgia grew up listening to the adventure novels of James Fenimore Cooper, *The Arabian Nights*, and tales of cowboys and Indians in the Wild West.

As she grew older, Georgia enjoyed exploring her parents' farm, which spanned 440 acres in 1890. She learned to appreciate the land and the changes it underwent during the passing seasons. She studied the local wildflowers, listened to the songs of the birds, and examined the checkerboard patterns made by her father's carefully cultivated fields.

Shortly before her fifth birthday, Georgia began attending school in Sun Prairie's one-room schoolhouse. One of her teachers remembered her as a "little, dark-skinned, wide-eyed, sprite-like child." Although she later remarked that she disliked school, the quiet little girl kept her feelings hidden. Georgia was a well-behaved child, a good student, and an enthusiastic participant in schoolyard games. She also enjoyed rambling alone on her family's farm, but as she grew older she gave up some of her explorations to spend time studying and helping with household chores. She later said that she "was the type of selfdisciplined child who liked to save the raisin in the cookie for the last because it was the best."

When Georgia was about 12, she and her sisters began taking private art lessons in their home. They spent evenings copying spheres, cubes, and other geometric shapes out of a drawing textbook. The next year, the O'Keeffe girls began receiving painting lessons from a local artist named Sarah Mann. At first Georgia was content to make watercolor copies of book illustrations, choosing such subjects as horses and roses. Gradually, however, she began to experiment, striving to capture the subtle hues of sunlight and shadow with paint.

The entire O'Keeffe family saw that Georgia had a talent for art. Although her mother encouraged her—perhaps hoping that she would one day become an art instructor—no one believed that Georgia could make her living as a painter. At that time, few young women ever contemplated such a thing.

Georgia, however, had other ideas. While playing with a friend one day, the two girls began talking about the future. Twelve-year-old Georgia surprised her friend—and herself—when she announced that she wanted to be an artist when she grew up. O'Keeffe later described her early feelings about

As a child, O'Keeffe had many outlets for her imagination. She made a house and costumes for her china dolls, which were similar to the one shown in this 1836 painting, Girl with Doll.

art: "I decided that the only thing I could do that was nobody else's business was to paint. I could do as I chose because no one would care."

In 1901, Georgia enrolled in Sacred Heart Academy, a boarding school run by Catholic nuns on the outskirts of Madison. Mr. O'Keeffe was Catholic, but Georgia had been raised in her mother's Protestant church. Her religious background was not a problem, however, because the academy accepted non-Catholic students. Initially, Georgia was unhappy at the school. The nuns were often strict, and she was crowded into a dormitory with the

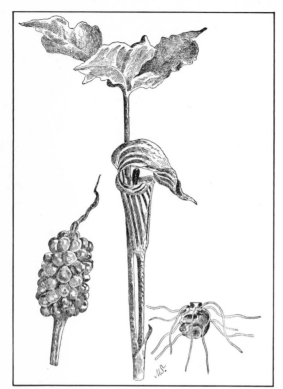

After her high-school art teacher brought a jack-in-the-pulpit plant into the classroom, O'Keeffe became more aware of the colors and shapes found in nature.

Georgia cried over this apparent failure. But she was an adaptable girl; she soon modified her technique enough to satisfy her teacher and win a gold pin for "improvement in illustration and drawing" at the end of the year.

Back at home, change was brewing. Although the farm provided a good living, Frank O'Keeffe wanted to leave Wisconsin. All three of his brothers had died of tuberculosis there, and he feared he would be next if he did not get away from Wisconsin's harsh, cold winters. He decided to sell the farm and move to Williamsburg, Virginia, which had a gentler climate.

Probably because the family could not afford private school tuition for their three older daughters at the same time, the O'Keeffes took Georgia out of Sacred Heart in 1902 and sent Ida and Anita in her place. Georgia and her brother Francis went to live in Madison with an aunt, while her parents and the three younger children moved to Virginia.

Georgia attended Madison High School that year, where she continued to do well in her studies. In her autobiography, O'Keeffe described her most memorable experience there, which took place when her art teacher showed the students a jack-in-the-pulpit, a wildflower Georgia had often seen on her father's farm. "Holding a Jack-in-the-pulpit high, she pointed out the strange shapes and variations in color—from the deep, almost black

other students. She missed her indulgent parents and her room at home, which was situated in a tower with big windows that overlooked the plains. But she quickly grew to enjoy life at Sacred Heart, especially because the curriculum emphasized the arts.

On the first day of drawing class, one of the nuns criticized Georgia's charcoal sketch of a baby's hand, saying that it was too small and too dark. Unaccustomed to sharp criticism, earthy violet through all the greens. . . . I was a little annoyed at [myself for] being interested because I didn't like the teacher. . . . But maybe she started me looking at things—looking very carefully at details." After that demonstration, Georgia realized that living things could be used as models, that there could be more to art than copying from book illustrations or plaster casts. Years later, Georgia would do her own series of paintings based on the jack-in-the-pulpit.

At the end of the school year, the eldest O'Keeffe children joined the family in Williamsburg, where Mr. O'Keeffe had purchased land and opened a grocery store. The family moved into a grand 18-room house, which remained sparsely furnished the entire time they lived there. As biographer Laurie Lisle noted in her book on O'Keeffe, "At the time, it was unusual for strangers to settle in Williamsburg, and the 'odd' Yankee ways of the O'Keeffes stood out. For one thing, neighbors noted, they didn't have black servants like the rest of white Williamsburg. For another, few of them ever went to church. Georgia, particularly, seemed out of place. She made no great effort to be sociable in the Southern style and did not dress or act like a sweetly submissive Virginia belle."

That fall, Georgia attended Chatham Episcopal Institute, a well-regarded girls' boarding school 200 miles away.

In such works as July 15, *American painter Grant Wood captured midwestern landscapes similar to the rolling fields of southern Wisconsin, O'Keeffe's childhood home.*

The school provided a rigorous education in a simple, almost spartan, environment. As she had in Williamsburg, Georgia stood out. Christine McRae, a classmate, later commented that Georgia's "features were plain—not ugly, for each one was good, but large and unusual-looking. She would have made a strikingly handsome boy." McRae also remembered O'Keeffe's "exuberance and enthusiasm," although she noted that "the most unusual thing about her was the absolute plainness of her attire."

Unmindful of what her classmates thought of her appearance, Georgia made friends easily. She impressed them with her artistic skills, expertly sketching their profiles and then tossing the drawings away as if they meant

O'Keeffe attended the Art Institute of Chicago from 1905 to 1906. Undaunted by the school's highly competitive environment, she ranked first in her class after only one semester there.

nothing at all. She used her good sense of humor to put the other girls at ease. Georgia could also be arrogant at times, and she was not above ordering her classmates around on occasion. As she asked Christine McRae, "When so few people think at all, isn't it all right for me to think for them and get them to do what I want?"

Elizabeth May Willis, an art teacher who also served as Chatham's principal, immediately recognized Georgia's talent as an artist. Although Georgia was sometimes distracted or boisterous in class, Mrs. Willis defended her, telling her detractors, "When the spirit moves Georgia, she can do more in a day than you can do in a week." Understanding that Georgia needed to work at her own pace, Willis let her set her own schedule in the art studio.

When she graduated from Chatham, Willis awarded her a special diploma in art and a prize for a lively watercolor depicting red and yellow corn.

After Georgia's graduation from Chatham in 1905, her mother and Mrs. Willis urged her to develop her talent further at an art school. In September she moved to Illinois to live with her mother's sister and brother and to attend the prestigious Art Institute of Chicago.

Although a part of one of the country's most active art museums, the school at the Art Institute did not encourage students to develop a uniquely American style of painting. At that time, the instructors considered Paris the art capital of the world, and students were taught in accordance with the tough, competitive French system. Each month, the instructor publicly ranked the students' work. Then he allowed the students with the highest numbers to sit in the best seats.

Unintimidated by this competitive environment, Georgia buckled down and applied herself to her studies. In October, after a month of classes, Georgia ranked fourth out of 44 beginning students and was moved into an intermediate group. By February of 1906, she ranked first in that class.

She found her courses easy—except for her anatomy class. One day a male model—naked except for a loincloth—posed for the class. As she later recorded in her autobiography, she was shocked and surprised: "I don't know why it seemed so difficult. In the summer when we went swimming a boy my age wore the least little piece of a bathing suit and I don't remember thinking anything about it except that he was blond and beautiful and laughing. The bare figure in that dismal dark cloakroom with everybody else dressed was different—he was definitely there to be looked at."

Despite her embarrassment, she endured the anatomy class because it was required. But throughout her career, O'Keeffe never displayed much interest in painting the human figure. She was more interested in the bold shapes and vivid colors that existed both in nature and in her keen imagination.

In June, Georgia returned to her family's home. Her father had believed Williamsburg to be a healthier environment, but he had traded Wisconsin's bitter winters for Virginia's hot, muggy summers. Georgia was stricken with typhoid fever, a life-threatening disease that was not uncommon in the southern city. Her family feared she might die, but she pulled through by the end of September. Her high fever left her temporarily bald, and she was very weak for a long time afterward.

An art student copies a painting in New York's Metropolitan Museum of Art. O'Keeffe completed many such exercises in the course of her art education.

Her health still fragile, Georgia remained in Virginia to recuperate. She began painting again, at an easel set up in the yard. As she grew stronger, she planned to return to school.

This time, however, she went not to Chicago but to New York City. Georgia wanted to study at the Art Students League, the alma mater of Elizabeth Willis, the headmistress of Chatham Episcopal Institute. New York would soon expose the young artist to a multitude of exciting new thoughts and experiences.

O'Keeffe's unconventional beauty inspired many artists, including Alfred Stieglitz, who took this photograph. At New York's Art Students League, her fellow students often asked her to pose for them.

THREE

Breakthrough

Georgia O'Keeffe arrived in New York City in 1907. After spending so much time bedridden in Williamsburg with a serious illness, she reveled in the freedom she found in New York, a city alive with ideas and sensations new to the developing young artist. She rented an inexpensive room near the Art Students League on West 57th Street and soon made friends with many of her classmates, a high-spirited group of young people who enjoyed all the pleasures the growing metropolis had to offer them. O'Keeffe's outlook brightened in their company.

Her classes at the league suited O'Keeffe's artistic temperament better than had those at the institute in Chicago. She enrolled in William Merritt Chase's class on portraits and still lifes. A dapper man with a passionate enthusiasm for American art, he encouraged his students to paint with bright colors and rapid brush strokes. He insisted that his pupils make a painting a day, using the same canvas over and over until it was too encrusted with paint to work with anymore. Like many of her classmates, O'Keeffe found his personality, teaching methods, and ideas invigorating. She later commented that whenever he entered the school, "a rustle seemed to flow from the ground floor to the top that 'Chase has arrived!'"

Other students often asked O'Keeffe to let them paint her portrait. She did not think of herself as beautiful, but others found her features intriguing. There was something about her well-shaped head, strong chin, wavy brown hair, and slightly secretive smile that made her fellow students want to capture her on canvas.

One classmate, Eugene Speicher, stopped her in the hallway one day after O'Keeffe had refused to sit for him, not wanting to cut a class. Barring her way, Speicher said, "It doesn't matter what you do. I'm going to be a great painter, and you will probably end up teaching painting in some girls' school."

O'Keeffe never forgot his prediction, which she hoped would not come true. Eventually, she did pose for Speicher. In fact, his portrait of O'Keeffe won him a fifty-dollar prize and still hangs today in the Member's Room at the league. But O'Keeffe, who would become one of America's most famous painters, had the last laugh.

That winter, a show of some drawings by French sculptor Auguste Rodin caused a stir in the New York art world. With their apparently simple pencil lines and light washes of watercolor, the drawings seemed crude and ugly to the members of the art establishment, perhaps a prank on the part of the artist, who was celebrated for the lifelike quality of his massive sculptures.

O'Keeffe and a group of her friends set off to make up their own minds. The drawings did not impress O'Keeffe, but the event afforded her her first glimpse of the 291 gallery and its controversial owner, Alfred Stieglitz. "I very well remember the fantastic violence of Stieglitz's defense when the students with me began talking with

him about the drawings," O'Keeffe recalled. "I had never heard anything like it, so I went into the farthest corner and waited for the storm to be over."

At the end of the year, O'Keeffe's months of diligent study in Chase's class paid off when she won the top still-life prize. Her painting depicted a dead brown rabbit lying beside a copper pot, and it earned O'Keeffe $100. More importantly, O'Keeffe received an invitation to attend the league summer school at Lake George, New York. She eagerly accepted and continued to hone her painting skills in the lovely wooded setting.

While things had gone well for her during the school year and summer, O'Keeffe found only hardship awaiting when she returned home in the fall. Her father's grocery store, feed business, and other financial ventures had failed, and the family now had trouble making ends meet. O'Keeffe understood that there was no extra money to send her back to New York.

Deciding it was time she supported herself, the 21-year-old O'Keeffe moved to Chicago to live with some of her mother's relatives. She landed a job as a free-lance illustrator, working on newspaper advertisements. Having learned to work quickly at the Art Students League, she succeeded in her trade but found the daily routine numbingly mindless, the city depressing and crowded. Then a bout with measles temporarily weakened her eyesight so much that she could no longer do intricate illustration. After two years in Chicago O'Keeffe returned to Virginia.

The O'Keeffe family had not fared well during Georgia's absence. Still in debt, they were now faced with the knowledge that Ida O'Keeffe had tuberculosis, the very ailment her husband left Wisconsin to avoid. As the disease attacked her lungs, it left Mrs. O'Keeffe completely exhausted. She rarely ventured downstairs anymore, and she spent her days and nights sleeping on the porch outside her bedroom. Soon she left Williamsburg for Charlottesville, a town in the cooler, mountainous part of the state, where she hoped to regain her health.

O'Keeffe's favorite instructor, William Merritt Chase, addresses a class at the Art Students League. She later described him as "fresh and energetic and fierce and exacting."

This still life depicting a rabbit and a copper pot earned O'Keeffe a $100 prize from the league in 1908. Several years later, she would abandon representational art to explore her own inner vision.

Twenty-three years old, with few prospects in Williamsburg, O'Keeffe stopped painting, uncertain as to what she might do next with her life. Her mentor from Chatham, Elizabeth May Willis, came to her rescue. Disappointed that O'Keeffe had given up her art, the headmistress arranged to take a leave of absence from the school so that O'Keeffe could teach art in her place.

In 1912, O'Keeffe's father decided to move to Charlottesville to be with his wife and open a creamery. The five O'Keeffe sisters now lived at home, and Anita and young Ida attended summer school at the nearby University of Virginia. Anita, who was very interested in drawing, enrolled in a class taught by Alon Bement, an assistant professor of fine arts at Columbia University Teachers College in New York. Anita liked

In Charlottesville, Virginia, Anita (left) and Ida (right) O'Keeffe attended the University of Virginia. Georgia (below) joined them, enrolling in Alon Bement's drawing class.

this professor's interesting notions about art, and so she urged her older sister Georgia to attend a class with her. There, the sisters learned about a new kind of art.

Until the end of the 19th century, most fine art was "representational." That is, artists strove to depict objects as they appeared. Whether the subject was a bowl of fruit, a king, or even a mythological creature, the painter rendered the scene in as lifelike a manner as possible.

Young Woman Reading a Letter *by Dutch artist Jan Vermeer typifies the representational painting admired by the art establishment before the rise of modernism.*

In the 1870s, however, a group of French painters began experimenting with new ways of depicting reality, ways that took into account both an object's appearance and the perceptions of the viewer. The Impressionists, as they were called, painted tangible objects, but their painting technique, which involved applying hundreds of discrete dabs of color to the canvas, simulated the way that light is reflected from surfaces. The Impressionists believed that by depicting objects as *they* saw them, they could invoke a similar emotional reaction in the viewer.

In the early years of the 20th century, some painters moved even farther away from representational art by painting abstract figures, shapes, and patterns that existed only within their own minds. Alon Bement was interested in this new form of art, and O'Keeffe was ready to hear his ideas. Representational painting, at which she had excelled in school, had lost its allure. "If one could only reproduce nature," she asked herself, "and always with less beauty than the original, why paint at all?"

Bement worked in New York with Arthur Wesley Dow, an instructor who had devised a new method for teaching drawing. Instead of drawing objects from nature or copying the works of the masters, the Dow method encouraged students to experiment with nonrepresentational shapes and patterns as they learned about basic concepts of composition and balance.

O'Keeffe found the Dow method immensely liberating. She had grown tired of painting what people told her to paint. She longed to capture abstract feelings on paper and canvas, and here was a theory that suggested her goal might indeed be attainable. O'Keeffe enrolled in Bement's most advanced summer class.

One day she received a telegram from a friend in Texas, telling her

Claude Monet, the great Impressionist, created The Houses of Parliament *using techniques developed in the late 19th century.*

about a winter teaching position in Amarillo. O'Keeffe accepted the offer; she was eager for new challenges and landscapes. "Texas had always been a sort of far-away dream," O'Keeffe wrote in her autobiography. "It had always seemed to me that the West must be wonderful—there was no place I knew of that I would rather go—so when I had a chance to teach there—off I went to Texas—not knowing much about teaching."

In 1912, Amarillo was still a rugged cattle town, a far cry from genteel Virginia or sophisticated New York. O'Keeffe, however, enjoyed its wildness. The vastness of the surrounding plains made a great impression on her. She learned to appreciate the unpredictability and fierceness of the

35

weather there, including tornadoes and dust storms. She found something pure and challenging in the bleak, vivid landscape. As she later said, "That was my country—terrible winds and wonderful emptiness."

O'Keeffe had her work cut out for her in Amarillo. Her official title was "supervisor of drawing and penmanship," and she was expected to teach art to hundreds of pupils throughout the Amarillo school system. But she found herself nearly as invigorated by this challenge as she was by the dramatic Texas landscape.

One day, she and her students hoisted a live pony onto her desk. She told the children to draw the animal. Remembering what had most influenced her artistic growth, she wanted her students to learn to draw subjects from nature, instead of copying figures from books.

As much as the children enjoyed these lessons, O'Keeffe's colleagues did not approve of such nontraditional methods. Many of them also considered O'Keeffe eccentric and unsociable because she preferred to board at the Magnolia Hotel rather than at a boardinghouse with other teachers. The rowdy hotel provided O'Keeffe with a glimpse of the "wild West." Laurie Lisle described the hotel in her book *Portrait of An Artist: A Biography of Georgia O'Keeffe*:

> The Magnolia's dining room was popular with the ravenous cowboys fresh from the cattle drives whose lips were blistered by the sun and eyes were bloodshot from the wind. Georgia watched with amazement as they wolfed down two or three complete dinners in one sitting. Hard drinkers, old-timers, loose women, and card sharks also frequented the hotel, and she heard vivid talk about outlaws, cattle rustlers, and violent frontier justice.

During the summer of 1913, O'Keeffe returned to Charlottesville to assist Bement at the University of Virginia summer school. Avidly interested in her career, the professor critiqued her work, offered encouragement, and introduced her to the theories of Wassily Kandinsky, the Russian artist credited with creating the first abstract paintings. In his book, *Concerning the Spiritual in Art*, Kandinsky connected visual art to music and discussed the psychological effects of color. "Generally speaking, color directly influences the soul," he wrote. "Color is the keyboard, the eyes are the hammer, the soul is the piano with many strings. The artist is the hand that plays, touching one or another purposively, to cause vibrations in the soul." O'Keeffe took many of Kandinsky's theories to heart, especially those about color and form. Later in her career, she painted abstractions inspired by music.

Bement urged her to study with Dow at Columbia Teachers College. As much as she loved the Texas plains, the idea of returning to New York grew more attractive to O'Keeffe as she became embroiled in a controversy over

Wassily Kandinsky's work demonstrates a complex interplay of shape and color. The Russian painter's theories about art strongly influenced O'Keeffe.

her teaching methods. The Amarillo school board demanded that she use specified texts to conduct her classes, but O'Keeffe refused to comply. In the summer of 1914, she finally quit her job in Amarillo so that she could attend Columbia Teachers College in the fall.

37

O'Keeffe threw herself into her studies, trying to soak up as many new ideas as possible. As Anita Pollitzer, the classmate who later showed O'Keeffe's work to Stieglitz, commented, "There was something insatiable about her— as direct as an arrow and hugely independent." She opened herself to the intriguing theories of Arthur Dow, who encouraged her to experiment with her painting as much as she desired. It was during this time that she became interested in Stieglitz's 291 gallery, which was regularly exhibiting groundbreaking artworks by then-controversial artists such as Picasso and Cézanne.

But, unable to afford life in the big city, O'Keeffe left New York after one year and took a job at a teachers college in Columbia, South Carolina. There she made the first bold breakthrough that demonstrated how truly special her talent was.

That fall, O'Keeffe felt dissatisfied with her projects. One day in October, she locked herself in her studio and analyzed her most recent drawings and paintings. She studied each carefully, trying to remember what had inspired her to undertake each piece. She noticed that many were influenced by other painters; others were done in styles calculated to please her instructors. After much introspection, she decided that there were abstract forms in her imagination unlike any she had ever seen on paper or canvas.

O'Keeffe recalled, "I could think of a whole string of things I'd like to put down but I'd never thought of doing it because I'd never seen anything like it." She did not know where these personal visions came from, but she made up her mind to paint them.

Determined to start anew, she put her earlier artwork in storage and began a process she later said was "like learning to walk." Each night after her classes, she spread cheap sketch paper on the floor and drew on it with charcoal until her hands ached. She worked at a fever pitch, alternating between joy and despair, finding intense pleasure in the powerful and unusual images conjured from her imagination but wondering whether they might be a symptom of mental illness.

Drawing XIII, for example, features violent zigzags, bulbous shapes like sooty fingerprints, and a wavy band of light and dark, all crowded together at the center of the paper and thrusting upward. In drawings that later served as drafts for the watercolor *Blue Lines X*, O'Keeffe attached two thin, parallel, vertical lines (one angled at the top) to a thick, dark, horizontal base. Some observers later interpreted this piece as symbolizing the relationship between men and women.

It was these drawings that O'Keeffe sent to Anita Pollitzer and that impressed Stieglitz so profoundly. Stieglitz and O'Keeffe soon began a correspondence. At the first opportunity, she left South Carolina for New York. There she had her confrontation with Stieglitz after she discovered her drawings were on display at 291 without her permission.

Georgia's mother met a tragic death that May. When the landlady came to collect the overdue rent and demanded to see Mrs. O'Keeffe, the desperately ill woman dragged herself out of bed. As she made her way to the front door, her lungs hemorrhaged, and she collapsed and died. Her death shattered the O'Keeffe clan. In the following years, the children went their separate ways and rarely saw each other.

In September of 1916, O'Keeffe began teaching at West Texas State Normal College in Canyon, a small town 20 miles south of Amarillo. She managed to fire many of her students with her passion for beauty, opening their eyes to the natural wonders that abounded in the surrounding prairies. "She was a good teacher," one student recalled. "There was a strength to her teaching—she knew what she thought and she expressed it."

O'Keeffe spent a good deal of her own time exploring the wide, wild, open spaces, wandering through the canyons, watching the sun and the changing sky. The country around Canyon inspired her to begin painting

Discarding many of the conventional elements of painting, O'Keeffe began working with imaginary forms in 1915, producing such daring paintings as Blue Lines X *(1916).*

with color again. Because she had little spare time, she worked in watercolors, which dry quickly and do not require much preparation or cleanup.

O'Keeffe observed the shapes found in nature and translated them into very personal abstractions. Instead of depicting a hill in meticulous, realistic detail, she filled the paper with a blotch of bright blue set off by a hint of washed-out sky, as in *Blue Hill #2*. She

Evening Star III, *painted in 1917, is one of a series O'Keeffe made at West Texas State Normal College, where she taught art.*

also experimented with color, mixing interesting combinations and using varying amounts of water to give her work different textures. O'Keeffe's best-known works from her time in Canyon include a series of 10 watercolors of the evening star, painted in bold swathes of red, blue, and yellow.

During her time in Canyon, O'Keeffe maintained her correspondence with Stieglitz. On April 3, 1917, he opened her first solo show at 291. A reviewer for the *Christian Science Monitor* expressed the prevalent critical opinion of her work—puzzlement and awe:

The interesting but little-known personality of the artist . . . is perhaps the only real key, and even that would not open all the chambers of the haunted place which is a gifted woman's heart. . . . Her strange art affects people variously and some not at all . . . artists especially wonder at its technical resourcefulness for dealing with what hitherto has been deemed the inexpressible—in visual form, at least. . . .

Three days after the opening, the United States declared war on Germany and entered World War I. The war affected Stieglitz deeply; he felt his loyalty torn between his native land, the U.S., and Germany, the country where he had learned much of his photographic craft. Depressed, and exhausted after years of nonstop toil, Stieglitz prepared to close 291.

Aware of Stieglitz's poor spirits and wishing to see her own show, O'Keeffe impulsively left Canyon as soon as classes were over, taking the long, hot train ride to New York. When she arrived, Stieglitz rehung her exhibit for her and introduced her to other artists. He also photographed her, something he did only with people to whom he felt close. O'Keeffe enjoyed a few hectic and invigorating days with him in the city and then returned to Texas.

Later that summer, O'Keeffe and her younger sister Claudia, who had come to live with her in Canyon, visited Santa Fe, New Mexico. O'Keeffe immediately fell in love with the town, marveling at the bright desert light, the simplicity of the adobe huts and the bright garments of the Indian residents. She vowed that she would someday return to New Mexico.

War fever now raged in Canyon as in the rest of the country. The townspeople were eager to outdo each other in their displays of patriotism. O'Keeffe, by inclination a pacifist, found their excesses disturbing. The townspeople, in turn, could not understand her wish to ignore the war and be left alone to teach her students.

In December, when her sister left to student teach in another community, O'Keeffe felt her spirits sag, and she stopped painting. As winter set in, the temperature tumbled below zero. O'Keeffe stuffed newspapers into her clothes as insulation against the bitter winds but nevertheless caught a case of influenza. The flu was not to be taken lightly then: Over half a million Americans died of it that year alone. In February, she took a leave of absence from the college and headed for a friend's farm in the warmer, southern part of the state.

Meanwhile, Stieglitz embarked on a campaign to bring O'Keeffe back to New York. He worried about her health and encouraged her to continue painting. O'Keeffe resisted the entreaties in his letters. In May, Stieglitz sent Paul Strand, a young photographer and mutual friend, to "rescue" O'Keeffe from Texas.

O'Keeffe gave the proposal a great deal of thought. She loved Texas, with its wild and unpredictable landscapes. But her experience with the conservative, judgmental citizens of Canyon made her question whether she could be happy there. She appreciated everything Stieglitz had done for her as her mentor, and she longed to work more closely with him. Finally, in June 1918 she gave in and joined Strand on the train back to New York, back to Alfred Stieglitz.

Black Flower and Blue Larkspur *(1929). O'Keeffe said, "I have used these things to say what is to me the wideness and wonder of the world as I live in it."*

FOUR

Flowers and Skyscrapers

In New York, Stieglitz set O'Keeffe up in his niece's apartment at 114 East Fifty-ninth Street. As the weeks passed, he and O'Keeffe began spending more and more time together. The attraction they felt toward each other was obvious to all who knew the couple. To those who inquired about their closeness, however, Stieglitz contended that O'Keeffe was merely a young artist whose talent he wished to encourage.

Stieglitz was married, and had a teen-aged daughter. His wife, Emmy, a brewery heiress, supported his career financially, but she had little understanding of art, modern or otherwise. She shared none of her husband's intense passion for photography, and theirs had not been a happy marriage. Neither of them, however, had taken the step of filing for divorce, then a long and complicated process. Until

fairly recently, societal norms and the legal system prevented couples from separating as easily as they do today.

That summer, Stieglitz took O'Keeffe with him to Oaklawn, his family's estate on Lake George in the Adirondack Mountains. During their stay, the couple openly displayed their affection for each other, luxuriating in the relaxed atmosphere of the country retreat. Other members of the family, especially Stieglitz's mother, Hedwig, did not begrudge them their happiness. Feeling that Stieglitz and his wife had been mismatched from the very beginning, they welcomed O'Keeffe into the family.

Fall came, and Stieglitz moved in with O'Keeffe. He later commented, "O'Keeffe came along and we found we were co-workers. We believed in the same things and finally we lived to-

Emmy and Kitty Stieglitz, the photographer's wife and daughter, were powerless to prevent the romance that developed between Stieglitz and O'Keeffe.

gether." He certainly did not wish to see O'Keeffe return to her teaching position in Texas. He did not want her to leave him, and he was convinced that the time O'Keeffe spent teaching would be better spent working in the studio.

There was, however, the question of how she could support herself. O'Keeffe still did not believe that she could earn a living from her paintings. Collectors were skeptical about modern art in 1918, and women painters were not taken seriously as artists.

Stieglitz certainly could not support her. As he later said, "I already knew I loved her, but I also knew I was an old man and I couldn't take care of a woman and a family." However, he managed to secure a $1,000 loan from a friend, enough for O'Keeffe to live on for at least a year. She abruptly resigned from her post at West Texas State Normal College and remained in New York.

Those first years with Stieglitz were some of O'Keeffe's happiest. The photographer and the painter seemed to complement each other well. He prized O'Keeffe for her intelligence, outspokenness, and artistic integrity. She, in turn, learned much from Stieglitz, benefiting from his vast experience in the Manhattan art world. She enjoyed his company and shared his devotion to beautiful things. The two of them would often be inspired by the same subjects: clouds, hillsides, building details. Sometimes a good-natured rivalry emerged as they competed to claim a particular object or landscape for their own. "Once Stieglitz got ahead of me," O'Keeffe recalled later: "He shot a door before I could paint it."

O'Keeffe's work from this period reflected her happiness. Brightly colored abstract paintings such as *Music Pink and Blue* (1919) seemed to emanate a fresh, sensual energy that some observers attributed to a newfound joy and zest for life.

Stieglitz, who had temporarily given

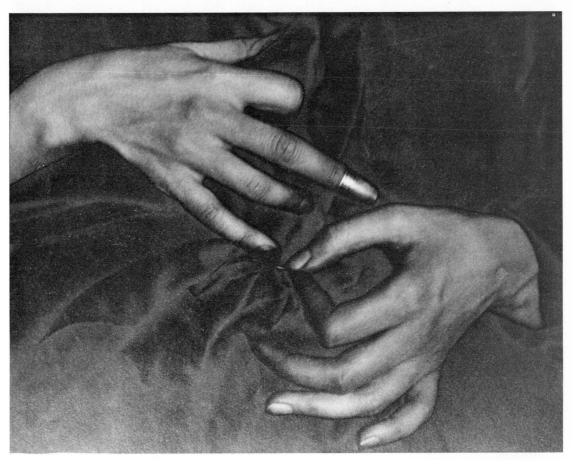

Georgia O'Keeffe (Hands and Thimble) *was one of the many photographs that Stieglitz took of O'Keeffe during their first years together. Much later, he still found her an intriguing subject.*

up photography, was also inspired by their relationship. He began taking pictures of O'Keeffe in a variety of poses: serious, clownish, erotic. He took close-up photos of her hands, lips, eyes, neck—even her feet.

In 1921, Mitchell Kennerly, the president of Anderson Galleries, a well-known art auction house on Park Avenue, offered to host a retrospective exhibition of Stieglitz's photographs. Of the 145 photos selected, 45 featured O'Keeffe. The show caused an imme-diate sensation. Because Stieglitz often posed O'Keeffe in front of her own work, observers saw that his model was a talented artist. It was just as obvious how deeply Stieglitz felt for her. Everyone wanted to know more about the mysterious, striking Georgia O'Keeffe. "Mona Lisa got but one portrait of herself worth talking about," art critic Henry McBride noted. "O'Keeffe got a hundred. . . . Everybody knew the name. She became what is known as a newspaper personality."

O'Keeffe painted Lake George Window *(1929) during a stay at the Stieglitz family home in Lake George, New York. Stieglitz photographed this same window.*

Many of O'Keeffe's male contemporaries did not recognize the talent of women artists such as Mary Cassatt, who painted Lydia Crocheting in the Garden *in 1880.*

O'Keeffe got her own show at the Anderson in 1923. The works were untitled, identified only by date and number, but included paintings of fruit and flowers as well as abstractions inspired by music and spring. The show was a tremendous success. It established O'Keeffe as a remarkable talent in her own right; she was no longer overshadowed by her mentor and lover. O'Keeffe, however, was put off by all the attention lavished on her. She saw the necessity of exhibiting and selling her work, but she in no way enjoyed it.

Emmy Stieglitz, understanding that her marriage was over, finally divorced her husband in 1922. Stieglitz immediately began pressuring O'Keeffe to marry him. But, having lived with him since 1918, she saw no point in a formal ceremony, and resisted the idea. Eventually, Stieglitz managed to convince her, and the couple married on December 11, 1924. She was 37 years old, he was 61.

Although they suited each other well, inevitably there were conflicts. A steady stream of visitors came to see Stieglitz at their apartment, seeking the photographer's advice and encouragement. O'Keeffe, who valued solitude and privacy, sometimes found these guests intrusive and disruptive to her painting. She also had to fight to assert her credibility among them. "The boys," as she sarcastically referred to the male artists in Stieglitz's circle of friends, tended to dismiss offhandedly the work of any female artist, no matter how talented.

No one, however, got away with addressing O'Keeffe as "Mrs. Stieglitz." She later said, "I've hung on to [my name] with my teeth. I like getting what I've got on my own."

During their first years together, O'Keeffe and Stieglitz debated whether they should start a family. O'Keeffe enjoyed the company of small children, and she often said that she would like to be a mother. Because of his divorce, Stieglitz was not on good terms with his grown daughter, Kitty. He was not enthusiastic about starting over as a father late in life.

For O'Keeffe, it eventually came down to a choice between motherhood or a life devoted to art and Alfred Stieglitz. She chose to stay with Stieglitz, remain childless, and spend her days painting. No one can say for sure whether she ever regretted that decision. Some of her close friends, however, felt that O'Keeffe was better off without children, that her temperament was not suited to handle the stresses and strains of motherhood.

In 1924 O'Keeffe completed the first painting in a series that would add to her already considerable fame. She had always enjoyed painting flowers, but now she depicted a blossom of truly gigantic proportions, one that filled the canvas and seemed to reduce the viewer to the size of a bumblebee. No other artist had ever taken this approach. The flowers she painted were never totally realistic; rather than serving as botanical studies, they expressed her personal feelings about the flower. "I know I cannot paint a flower," O'Keeffe wrote, "but maybe in terms of paint color I can convey . . . my experience of the flower or the experience that makes the flower of significance to me at that particular time."

In the following years, she painted lilies, irises, daisies, orchids, and jack-in-the-pulpits, the flower she had seen a teacher use in an art lesson back at Madison High School. Art critics and the public responded to the paintings enthusiastically, and O'Keeffe's vibrant flowers were even used in advertising and product packaging. O'Keeffe said of her flower paintings, "When you take a flower in your hand and really look at it, it's your world for the moment. I want to give that world to someone else. Most people in the city rush around so, they have no time to

(Continued on page 57)

SELECTED WORKS
by GEORGIA O'KEEFFE

When, as a young artist, Georgia O'Keeffe resolved "to accept as true my own thinking," she laid the foundation for a career that both enriched and reflected the history of modern art. Removed from—yet informed by—the concerns of her contemporaries, O'Keeffe explored a unique personal vision centered on her belief that one cannot "separate the objective from the abstract." Representational painting, she said, "is not good painting unless it is good in the abstract sense. A hill or a tree cannot make a good painting just because it is a hill or a tree. It is lines and colors put together so that they say something. For me that is the very basis of painting. The abstraction is often the most definite form for the intangible thing in myself that I can only clarify in paint."

Three Eggs in a Pink Dish, ca 1928
oil on canvas, 12" x 31¾"
Museum of Fine Arts, Museum of New Mexico
From the Estate of Georgia O'Keeffe

Lake George, New York, ca 1924
oil on canvas, 8¾″ x 15¾″
Museum of Fine Arts, Museum of New Mexico
The Rebecca Salsbury James Collection

Desert Abstraction, 1931
oil on canvas, 15½″ x 36″
Museum of New Mexico Foundation

Blue River, 1935, oil on canvas, 16½″ x 30½″, Museum of Fine Arts
Museum of New Mexico. From the Estate of Georgia O'Keeffe

Red Hills and Pedernal, 1936
oil on canvas, 20″ x 30″
Museum of Fine Arts, Museum of New Mexico
Bequest of Helen Miller Jones

Spring Tree, No. 1, 1945
oil on canvas, 30″ x 36″
Museum of Fine Arts, Museum of New Mexico
From the Estate of Georgia O'Keeffe

In the Patio II, 1948
oil on canvas, 18″ x 30″
Museum of Fine Arts, Museum of New Mexico
Bequest of Helen Miller Jones

From the River—Light Blue, 1964
oil on canvas, 30″ x 40″
Museum of Fine Arts, Museum of New Mexico
From the Estate of Georgia O'Keeffe

(Continued from page 48)

look at a flower. I want them to see it whether they want to or not."

Some people found the giant flowers shocking, believing that the extreme close-ups of plant parts were references to human sexuality. (A woman who bought one of the flower paintings was upset to find someone using it to explain the facts of life to a child.) But O'Keeffe maintained that there was no conscious sexual content in her paintings, and pointed out that many male artists had painted flowers without having erotic imagery read into their work. In her opinion, if a viewer chose to see anything sexual in her paintings, that was his or her own concern and reflected in no way on O'Keeffe's own intentions.

In 1925, O'Keeffe and Stieglitz moved into the recently completed Shelton Hotel, one of New York City's first skyscrapers. The arrangement satisfied their domestic needs, the kitchen and maid service freeing them from much of the drudgery of day-to-day living. From the balcony of their top-floor room, O'Keeffe observed the construction of the skyscrapers springing up throughout Manhattan: the Chrysler Building, the Empire State Building, the American Radiator Building. She began painting them. At first, she met with resistance from Stieglitz, who did not think a woman from the midwestern prairies had the expertise to capture the complexities and energy of an emerging metropolis. When she sold

When he and O'Keeffe lived in the Shelton Hotel, one of New York's first skyscrapers, Stieglitz took this photograph of New York's burgeoning skyline.

her first New York picture for $1,200, Stieglitz admitted that he had been wrong.

In 5 years, O'Keeffe painted approximately 20 skyscrapers. The paintings displayed her mixed feelings about New York. Although they captured much of the excitement of living in a modern city, they also contained hints of menace and claustrophobia. For example, her *City Night*, painted in 1926, shows tall, dark buildings crowding a small white moon. *New York with Moon*, done the previous year, depicts

While living in New York, O'Keeffe found inspiration in the architecture of the growing city. She painted dozens of stark urban scenes.

a wan moon overpowered by a glaring streetlamp. Though often hauntingly beautiful, her city scenes are rarely friendly or inviting.

Her 1926 show created a sensation. "If ever there were a raging, blazing soul mounting to the skies it is that of Georgia O'Keeffe," the *New Yorker* commented. "One O'Keeffe hung in the Grand Central Station would even halt the home-going commuters... surely if the authorities knew they would pass laws against Georgia

O'Keeffe, take away her magic tubes and brushes."

In many of the paintings done during this period, O'Keeffe moved from realism to abstraction. At Lake George, where O'Keeffe and Stieglitz spent much of the year, she painted many scenes from nature, such as *Lake George, New York* (see page 50). She also began experimenting with still life, producing a range of images including *Three Eggs in a Pink Dish* (see page 49). One day, she picked up a loose shingle from a barn roof, brought it inside, and placed it against a wall with a white seashell in front of it. She then began a series of paintings based on the shingle and the shell. Several of them were realistic, but then, as O'Keeffe later wrote, "Finally I went back to the shingle and the shell—large again—the shingle just a dark space that floated off the top of the painting, the shell just a simple white shape under it. They fascinated me so that I forgot what they were except that they were shapes together—singing shapes."

O'Keeffe's reputation was boosted in 1928 when she sold a series of calla lily panels for an unprecedented sum. A French art collector, who has remained anonymous to this day, approached Stieglitz and inquired about the price of the paintings. Stieglitz, who believed that O'Keeffe's work should be sold only to the "right people," those who he believed truly appreciated her talent, offhandedly quoted the extravagant sum of $25,000, never suspecting that the Frenchman would accept. The collector agreed without an apparent second thought, paying a price equivalent to more than $200,000 today.

This sale was the talk of the New York art world for quite some time. People were impressed by the large amount of money involved and expressed surprise that someone from France—the supposed capital of the art world—would go to such a length to possess a painting by an American woman. "SHE PAINTED THE LILY AND GOT $25,000 AND FAME FOR DOING IT!" proclaimed the headline of a story in the New York *Evening Graphic*. The article's opening reflected the fact that many people were as fascinated by the artist as her work. It began, "Not a rouged, cigarette smoking, bob-haired, orange-smocked Bohemian, but a prim ex-country schoolmistress who actually does her hair up in a knot is the art sensation of 1928!"

As time passed, O'Keeffe began to tire of Lake George. At first she had enjoyed painting the region's woods, hills, water, and buildings, but as the years progressed, she resented spending so much time at the lake. She felt she had exhausted all possible subjects for painting there, and she also found it tiring to do all of the household chores, contend with hordes of in-laws for months on end, and find time for her own pursuits. But Stieglitz,

Overwhelmed by the demands of her growing fame and her ailing husband, O'Keeffe soon felt the need for a rest and a change of scenery.

now very set in his ways, would not hear of vacationing elsewhere.

The publicity from the sale of the calla lily paintings greatly upset O'Keeffe, who hated any commotion that forced her into the limelight. Not wishing to face another summer at Lake George after such a trying winter, she left on her own to visit relatives in Wisconsin. Upon her return, she found Stieglitz in poor health. In September 1928, he suffered a heart attack and required constant bed rest.

Because she spent a great deal of time tending to Stieglitz, O'Keeffe accomplished little new work that fall. Consequently, her 1929 exhibition at the Anderson proved a disappointment. Critics, whose expectations ran high after watching O'Keeffe successfully experiment with new techniques year after year, were for the most part gentle but unenthusiastic in their reviews, sensing correctly that the artist was undergoing a difficult emotional transition. Robert Coates of the *New Yorker* remarked that her style seemed too controlled, "the meticulousness showed a tendency to trip over itself, as one peering too closely at the minutiae before him might end by tripping over a matchstick."

Dorothy Brett, an English painter and a friend of O'Keeffe's, visited New York that year from Taos, New Mexico. She encouraged O'Keeffe to join her for the summer out west. O'Keeffe decided that it was indeed time for a vacation away from Stieglitz, who by now had sufficiently recovered from his illness to care for himself. Stieglitz did not like the idea, but his wife was insistent: She needed to find new inspiration for her art.

Now 41 years old, O'Keeffe had suffered through a lackluster show and found herself at a crossroads in her career. She set off on a new adventure in the place she loved best, the American West.

O'Keeffe appreciated the natural beauty of Lake George, but after several summers there she no longer found the lake and its environs stimulating.

O'Keeffe stands before one of her skull-and-flower paintings at her 1931 exhibition, entitled "Life and Death." After she first visited New Mexico, much of her art was inspired by the area's barren, haunting landscape.

FIVE

Desert Bones and Blooms

Soon after arriving in Santa Fe, New Mexico, O'Keeffe and her friend Rebecca "Beck" Strand attended a traditional corn dance at a nearby Indian village. There they encountered wealthy art patron Mabel Dodge Luhan and her Native American husband, Tony, both of whom they had met before in New York. After the performance, Mabel Luhan insisted that O'Keeffe and Strand accompany her to her home in Taos, a town that had in recent years become an artist's colony.

Luhan greatly enjoyed hobnobbing with writers and artists. British poet and novelist D. H. Lawrence, the author of *Sons and Lovers* and the controversial *Lady Chatterley's Lover*, visited her in Taos, as did novelist Willa Cather, author of *My Ántonia*. Although she pampered guests at the luxurious home, Luhan also tended to meddle in their private affairs. Her bossiness led some of the residents of Taos to sarcastically dub her "the Empress of Mabeltown."

Uncertain whether they wished to subject themselves to Luhan's somewhat intrusive personality, O'Keeffe and Strand did not give her a definite answer about visiting Taos. According to some reports, Luhan finally settled the issue by sending their baggage on ahead without them, leaving the women no choice but to follow.

Their insistent hostess set them up in a guest cottage near her own grand home. She also provided O'Keeffe with a studio, a small round building made of adobe bricks. Situated near a stream, with large windows providing dramatic views of a meadow and brooding Taos mountain, the studio soon proved to be a perfect spot for O'Keeffe

63

O'Keeffe enjoys a quiet moment outside the "Pink House," her Taos, New Mexico, residence, in 1929.

to paint the western scenes she had missed since she moved to New York.

In Taos, she rediscovered her joy for life. D. H. Lawrence had written that "in the magnificent fierce morning of New Mexico one sprang awake, a new part of the soul woke up suddenly"—a statement that was certainly true of O'Keeffe. She loved exploring the wild, unspoiled New Mexican terrain, finding pleasure in the silver-gray sagebrush, the purple mountains, and the vast expanses of desert. The landscape, which included hot springs and snow-covered peaks, fascinated her. The pure, radiant sunshine and the thin, dry air enabled her to see for miles on end and seemed to make everything she looked at beautifully simple and clear. For the first time in many months, O'Keeffe brimmed with energy and good spirits. According to Mabel Dodge Luhan, she frequently exclaimed, "Well! Well! Well! This is wonderful. No one told me it was like *this!*"

She also enjoyed meeting people who had no connection to Stieglitz's circle of New York friends. She found many of the writers and artists who visited Luhan in Taos fascinating. One individual with whom she struck up a friendship was a young Sierra Club photographer named Ansel Adams, later one of the best-known photographers of the American wilderness.

That summer, O'Keeffe also stayed with her friend Dorothy Brett at Kiowa

More than any other landscape, the deserts, hills, buttes, and mountains of New Mexico touched O'Keeffe and inspired her art.

The mission at Ranchos des Taos was a popular subject for many artists, including O'Keeffe. Although her interpretations of the building were highly original, some critics labeled these works "touristy."

Ranch. Mabel Dodge Luhan had given the ranch to D. H. Lawrence, who was away in Europe that year. One night, O'Keeffe lay on a bench beneath a massive pine tree and stared up through the branches at the star-filled sky. From memory, she later recreated that scene on canvas. The result, a work called *The Lawrence Tree*, became one of her favorite paintings.

Because she wanted the freedom to explore the deserts and mountains even more thoroughly, O'Keeffe purchased a black Model A Ford. One day while she and a friend, Charles Collier, were driving to Abiquiu, a small town 60 miles southwest of Taos, Collier pointed out the Ghost Ranch, a place he thought O'Keeffe might like to visit. Rumor had it that the ranch was strikingly beautiful—and haunted. She was intrigued, but they could not find the road that led down to it from the high plain on which they were driving. O'Keeffe's introduction to the Ghost Ranch, the place where she would one day do some of her best work, would have to wait.

During her travels in New Mexico, she occasionally encountered mysterious crosses that seemed to spring up from the arid landscape without rhyme or reason. Local residents told her that they were the work of the Penitentes, a secret religious society dating back to medieval Spain. Fascinated by the strange artifacts, O'Keeffe did a series of paintings featuring the crosses.

She also began a series of paintings based on the mission church at Ranchos des Taos. The 18th-century Spanish structure was a popular subject for artists in the area, but O'Keeffe depicted the mission in her own unique style, painting only fragments of it or rendering it as a giant mud-colored slab that seemed to rise up out of the earth itself beneath a turquoise sky.

If her spirits were high during that first summer in New Mexico, her husband's were not. Depressed at being separated from her and worried about her health, Stieglitz spent much of the summer writing to O'Keeffe. His anxiety-filled letters and telegrams so disturbed her that she offered to return to New York in July. Stieglitz, finally reassured that she did intend to come back to him, told her to stay as long as she needed.

O'Keeffe remained in New Mexico until August. When she arrived back in the East, she found Stieglitz in good health. Now 65 years old, Stieglitz still pursued new interests, which ranged from hiring a plane to fly him around Lake George to buying a Victrola (an early record player) so that he could enjoy the music of the classical composers Beethoven, Brahms, and Bach. O'Keeffe, content to be back with her husband, spent the autumn working on new paintings and finishing ones begun in Taos.

Several months after her return to New York, O'Keeffe, like millions of Americans, began to feel the effects of the stock market crash of October 1929. After the crash, the United States and many nations around the world rapidly descended into financial chaos. Businesses went bankrupt and over 10 million Americans suffered unemployment and poverty. The Great Depression had begun.

Although they knew that the depres-

A cross looms in the foreground of this photograph taken in New Mexico. Fascinated by the crosses erected by an obscure religious sect, O'Keeffe featured them in several paintings.

sion would adversely affect the art market, O'Keeffe and Stieglitz managed to remain calm and productive, resisting the panic that gripped so many other New Yorkers. In December, Stieglitz opened a new gallery at 509 Madison Avenue and called it An American Place. O'Keeffe was responsible for the spare, uncluttered look of the gallery, believing that the bright white walls, as well as the natural sunlight that flooded the space, would show artworks to their best advantage.

In February 1930, An American Place hosted O'Keeffe's new exhibition, featuring work from her trip to New Mexico. Many viewers were struck by the change in O'Keeffe's subject matter. While a few critics complained that the paintings of New Mexican crosses were "hysterical" and the church scenes too "touristy," most observers agreed that O'Keeffe's creativity had been fired by her western sojourn and that her new paintings were truly inspired.

The next month, O'Keeffe agreed to debate Michael Gold, the editor of the socialist magazine *New Masses*. Journalists and interested observers packed the dining room of a Manhattan hotel to watch them square off. Gold contended that art such as O'Keeffe's was decadent, that the working classes were the only appropriate subject for art. During the depression, many artists and critics thought as Gold did, but O'Keeffe told him, "You may be seeking the freedom of humanity, but you want to make art a tool—and the worst of it is that you must cheapen art to appeal to any mass, and your mass artists will inevitably become bad artists."

As a long-time feminist who had been involved in the movement to win woman suffrage years before (women nationwide had won the right to vote in 1920), O'Keeffe also asked Gold whether he included women on his list of oppressed groups that deserved

This 1920s photograph shows Abiquiu, New Mexico, a small town that O'Keeffe first visited in 1929. The Ghost Ranch, where she eventually settled, is outside Abiquiu.

to be championed in art. The radical turned out to be a conservative when it came to sexual equality. "I'm afraid it doesn't seem very important to me if the pampered *bourgeoise* in her rose-colored boudoir gets equal rights or not," he snapped. O'Keeffe calmly disagreed with his assertion that only working-class women were victimized by society, pointing out that she had long regretted that she had few female role models as she strove to develop her own style. She told Gold, "I am trying with all my skill to do a painting that is all of women, as well as all of me."

When O'Keeffe returned to New Mexico that summer, she once again had to contend with her husband's depression, possessiveness, and worsening hypochondria. Her life with Stieglitz became even more difficult that fall, thanks to the presence of Dorothy Norman, a young art enthusiast and writer in whom Stieglitz had begun to take a great interest.

Just as he had with O'Keeffe, Stieglitz took hundreds of photographs of Norman, going so far as to pose her in a black outfit similar to those worn by O'Keeffe. He also taught her the fundamentals of photography and arranged

Suffragists march in 1917. A supporter of the movement that won women's right to vote in 1920, O'Keeffe hoped "to do a painting that is all of women."

for the publication of some of her poems. She, in turn, helped Stieglitz with a variety of chores at the gallery, including bookkeeping and fund-raising.

Stieglitz's friendship with Norman infuriated O'Keeffe, who remembered how her own romance with the photographer had begun. She refused to speak to Norman. At social gatherings, she would not even stay in the same room with her. O'Keeffe wanted to be the only woman in Stieglitz's life. Upset and fearing that she was losing her husband, she was unable to paint throughout the winter of 1930–31. The following summer, she again traveled to New Mexico. There, she managed to resume her work, completing such paintings as *Desert Abstraction* (see page 51), but she stayed for just two months before she returned to her husband and the East Coast.

During her stays in New Mexico, O'Keeffe had taken great interest in the dry, bleached animal bones she found scattered across the desert. She gathered some up and shipped them off to Lake George. One day in 1931, she set a horse's skull on the dining room table, where a guest had left some blue pajamas. Later, while working with some fabric flowers, she was interrupted by a visitor. On impulse, she stuck a pink rose in one of the skull's eyes. As she later recalled, "On my return, I was so struck by the wonderful effect of the rose in the horse's eye that I knew that here was a painting that had to be done."

O'Keeffe's 1932 exhibition provided the art establishment with yet another shock. Some critics found the new series of skull-and-flower paintings sinister, morbid, even perverse. O'Keeffe did not see them that way. "When I found the beautiful white bones on the desert I picked them up and took them home," she wrote in her autobiography. "I have used these things to say what is to me the wideness and wonder of the world as I live in it." She also has said that "I was quite excited about our country" when she painted *Cow's Skull—Red, White, and Blue*. Its patriotic colors distinguished it as an emphatically American painting. Despite the controversy that was becoming customary for O'Keeffe's shows, the exhibition was another success. A critic for *Art News* raved, "What she will find to top this year's splendid salutation of the dead I cannot imagine, but it's a wide world and Miss O'Keeffe is not one to loiter along the way."

In 1932, O'Keeffe ventured farther into the "wide world," taking her first trip outside the United States. With Georgia Engelhard, Stieglitz's niece, she traveled to Canada, driving through the verdant farmland along the St. Lawrence River and to the rugged Gaspé coast. She made several

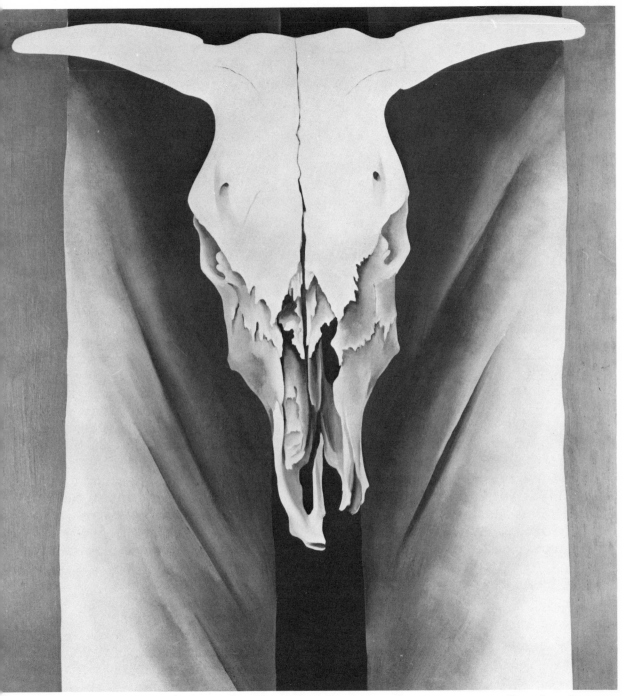

Many viewers were shocked by the juxtaposition of a skull with a patriotically-colored background in O'Keeffe's 1931 work Cow's Skull—Red, White, and Blue.

Stieglitz objected to O'Keeffe's intention to paint a mural for Radio City Music Hall, scene of popular musical spectacles and home of the famed Rockettes.

paintings during the trip, but the ocean did not speak to her with the same intensity that the desert had.

O'Keeffe and Stieglitz found themselves at odds that fall. She had been asked to paint a mural in the women's lounge of the newly built Radio City Music Hall. Stieglitz intensely disliked murals, believing that they cheapened fine art by pandering to popular tastes. He also objected to the fee for the project, a mere $1,500, several times less than the price of a single O'Keeffe oil. O'Keeffe, on the other hand, relished the chance to create a work on such a grand scale. Disregarding her husband's wishes, O'Keeffe signed a

contract. Ignoring his wife's decision, Stieglitz visited Donald Deskey, the director of the Radio City decoration project, and tried to break the contract. According to Deskey, he referred to O'Keeffe as "a child and not responsible for her actions." Deskey ignored the incident; the project would proceed as planned.

The mural was an enormous undertaking. The lounge contained hundreds of square feet of painting surface, much of it on the ceiling. O'Keeffe wanted to begin painting in August, but the canvas was not mounted on the walls until November. Radio City Music Hall was slated to open on December 27, 1932.

On the day she inspected the newly canvassed room, O'Keeffe saw that a section of fabric had become detached from the wall because workers had failed to secure it properly. This small setback must have released pent-up tensions, for O'Keeffe fled the building in tears.

The following day, Stieglitz told Deskey that O'Keeffe had suffered a nervous breakdown. He said she had been hospitalized, and would not be able to fulfill her contract. In fact, she was in seclusion at Lake George, but Deskey accepted Stieglitz's story and found another artist to paint the mural.

O'Keeffe returned to New York City in December. She was still nervous and depressed, and she suffered from frequent, painful headaches. Fearing

O'Keeffe portrayed the Southwest's undulating mountains in this 1930 work, Near Abiquiu, New Mexico.

that she might be losing her mind, she consulted doctors, who offered no real explanations for her distress.

Her condition worsened during January. O'Keeffe had trouble breathing. She could not eat, sleep, or even walk. Finally, on February 1 she was admitted to Doctors Hospital. Stieglitz's story about O'Keeffe's supposed nervous breakdown had become a reality.

O'Keeffe (left) greets an art collector at a 1940 Manhattan show. Although more comfortable painting and exploring the Southwest, she held her own in the New York art world.

SIX

The Road to Ghost Ranch

From February 1 to March 25, 1933, O'Keeffe remained in the hospital, where she gradually recovered her emotional and physical stability. The stress of planning her doomed mural for Radio City Music Hall surely contributed to her breakdown, but much of her mental torment stemmed from her strained relationship with Stieglitz.

At the age of 45, she was trying to balance her need to succeed as an artist with her sense of responsibility toward a husband who was nearly 70 years old. She felt that, although she was indebted to Stieglitz for helping launch her career, she also wanted to shine on her own. She understood Stieglitz's feelings of neglect during her trips to New Mexico, but she did not want to stop working in the place she loved best, a place he would not even visit. Then there was Stieglitz's con-

tinuing interest in Dorothy Norman. It had all been too much for O'Keeffe to handle.

Stieglitz had shown an exhibit of O'Keeffe's works, most of them done in previous years, while she was still in Doctors Hospital. Despite the scarcity of new pieces, her show drew the usual crowds. Art critic Ralph Flint called her paintings "ripe with beauty, touched by grace, buoyant with vision. . . ."

Following O'Keeffe's release from the hospital, Marjorie Content, an old friend, took her to Bermuda. The sun and solitude did much to improve the artist's health, but upon her return to New York, she displayed no desire to pick up her brushes again. She remained in this slump of inactivity well into the next year. Her 1934 show at An American Place was a retrospective of

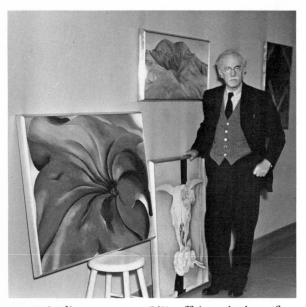

Stieglitz arranges O'Keeffe's paintings for a 1936 show. An astute judge of the art market, he helped cultivate his wife's reputation by exhibiting her works and negotiating their sale.

works done from 1915 to 1927, and was even more popular than her previous show. *Black Flower and Blue Larkspur*, a painting she had done in New Mexico years earlier, was sold to the Metropolitan Museum of Art. This sale helped bolster her reputation as an artist, and several others enabled O'Keeffe and Stieglitz to put money worries aside.

Her relationship with Stieglitz had improved after her breakdown. During her recovery, he had begun to understand that his behavior and attitudes had been partially responsibile for her illness. He had always admired and supported her work, but he could be sharply critical when she struck out on her own, as when she sought out an independent life in New Mexico instead of staying by his side in New York. As O'Keeffe biographer Laurie Lisle speculated, perhaps Stieglitz decided after her hospitalization that "whatever the price, he was committed to seeing her resume a full life of painting. Perhaps he realized that she had only defied him in order to survive as an artist."

In June of that year, she returned to New Mexico. It was a frightening decision—to set off alone again and face possible failure—but she resolved to do it, lest she waste her talent living safely beside Stieglitz. "I'm frightened all the time. Scared to death," she proclaimed years later. "But I've never let it stop me. Never!"

Back in New Mexico, O'Keeffe determined to learn more about the Ghost Ranch, the mysterious place she had been unable to find on her previous trip. While shopping in the town of Alcalde one day, she spotted a parked car with the initials "GR" painted on its side. When the driver returned to the car, O'Keeffe asked him whether he worked at Ghost Ranch. He did, and he gave her directions to the ranch, which was approximately 40 miles away.

She set out to find the ranch the next day. Driving her black Model A, she crossed the wooden bridge that spanned the Rio Grande, then followed a dirt road toward the town of Abiquiu. The farther she traveled across arroyos (water-carved channels) and wide plains surrounded by mountains and flat-topped hills, the wilder and more beautiful the terrain became. An animal skull marked the turn-off, and O'Keeffe soon came upon a group of ranch houses huddled beneath a golden mesa. She had found the Ghost Ranch.

Arthur Newton Pack, publisher of *Nature* magazine, owned the place and ran it as a dude ranch. For $80 a week—a large sum during the height of the Great Depression—wealthy pa-

O'Keeffe's friend Ansel Adams photographed this sign showing the way to her beloved Ghost Ranch. From the moment she first discovered the ranch in 1934, she spent much of her time there.

trons could stay in relative luxury while playing out their fantasies of the wild West. O'Keeffe thought the ranch was extraordinarily beautiful, but she did not particularly like its pampered clientele. She later joked, "I thought dude ranchers were a lower form of life." Nevertheless, she decided to return the next day for an overnight stay. She was assigned a room in Ghost House, the oldest building on the ranch. According to local superstition, a family had been murdered in the house years ago, and now a ghostly woman haunted the building by night, clutching a spectral infant in her arms.

O'Keeffe never saw any phantoms at Ghost Ranch, but the place entranced her nonetheless. She decided to move in, and she began exploring the surrounding desert in earnest. She hiked or drove miles each day, collecting a wide array of natural artifacts that interested her, mostly stones, branches, and bones.

She began painting again. The hills around Ghost Ranch particularly fascinated her. She enjoyed watching the way the sun and the clouds altered the color of the hills during the course of a day. Sometimes the cliffs glowed with pink and orange light; at other times they appeared to be red and purple. O'Keeffe strove to capture their color and texture on her canvases, painting alone from seven in the morning until five in the afternoon. During the hottest part of the day, she sometimes lay

Although her western sojourns meant long separations from her husband, O'Keeffe continued to travel to the region that inspired much of her best work.

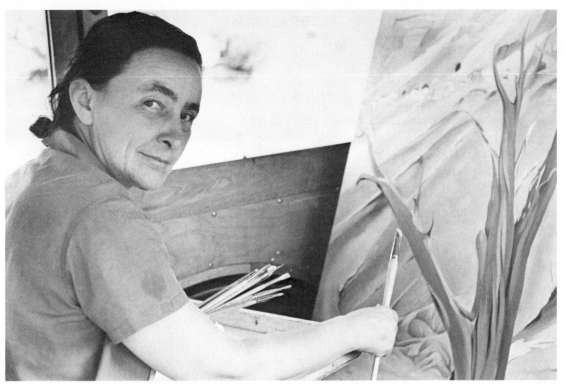

O'Keeffe paints in her car to escape the desert heat. Ansel Adams, who took this photograph, said of O'Keeffe, "Nobody can look at [her paintings] without being affected. So the mystique begins and endures."

in the only available shade, beneath her car.

O'Keeffe spent much of her time at the Ghost Ranch working in solitude. As Dorothy Brett remarked of her friend, "When you got to know Georgia, she was a very, very nice person. But she had a rather cold front that made things a little difficult for her and for everybody else. It's a horrid thing to say, but I think she was bored with people." She did develop friendships with some of the people she met at the ranch, those she considered suffi-

ciently intelligent, entertaining, or helpful. This category included the poet Spud Johnson and the Ghost Ranch's owner, Arthur Pack. She also renewed her acquaintance with Ansel Adams and, as the years went by, she would accompany him on several trips through the Indian country of western New Mexico and Arizona, as well as to California's dramatically beautiful Yosemite Valley.

At the end of the first summer, O'Keeffe asked Spud Johnson to drive her back to New York. For the next several years, she would spend her summers alone out west, and the rest of the year in New York City and Lake George with her husband. Each winter Stieglitz's An American Place would exhibit some of the paintings she had done the previous summer.

O'Keeffe painted some of her best-known work during her first years at Ghost Ranch. Her 1935 painting, *Blue River* (see page 52), and *Red Hills and Pedernal* (see page 53), painted in 1936, reflect her love of the Southwestern landscape made familiar to millions through her work. In *Ram's Head, White Hollyhock*, painted in 1935, a huge, precisely rendered skull and a delicate white-and-yellow flower float in an ominous gray sky over orange, tree-dotted hills. *New Yorker* critic Lewis Mumford called the painting "brilliant" and wrote, "Not only is it a piece of consummate craftsmanship, but it likewise possesses that mysterious force, that hold upon the hidden soul, which distinguishes important communication from the casual reports of the eye. . . ."

A majestic set of elk antlers looms over snow-covered mountains tinted blue and pink by an approaching dawn in O'Keeffe's 1937 painting *From the Faraway Nearby*. Like *Ram's Head, White Hollyhock*, this painting was interpreted by some viewers as a symbolic representation of the opposing forces of life and death, even of O'Keeffe's triumph over her recent ill-ness. O'Keeffe, leery of any psychological analysis of her work, insisted that, in the case of *Ram's Head*, the painting's elements "just sort of grew together."

In 1937, O'Keeffe arrived at Ghost Ranch without arranging for accommodations beforehand. When it turned out that no cottages were available, her host, Arthur Pack, set her up in Rancho de los Burros, a house a few miles from Ghost Ranch headquarters. The building was a simple adobe structure built around a patio. The bedroom window commanded a stunning view of nearby cliffs. With its secluded location, Rancho de los Burros was the perfect home for an artist so entranced by nature. "As soon as I saw it, I knew I must have it," O'Keeffe later remarked. "I can't understand people who want something badly but don't grab for it. I grabbed."

She moved in immediately, and found her surroundings a rich source of inspiration for her art. That summer, she did a painting of Rancho de los Burros entitled *The House I Live In*. She also depicted the Pedernal, a flat-topped mesa about 10 miles away, in a number of paintings. Years later she joked: "It's my private mountain. It belongs to me. God told me if I painted it enough, I could have it."

Although O'Keeffe now spent a good part of each year away from New York, the city remained the hub of her professional career—which was thriving.

An elk's skull and antlers hover over a New Mexican mountain sunrise in O'Keeffe's From the Faraway Nearby. *As she later said of such imagery, "The bones seem to cut sharply to the center of something that is keenly alive."*

Photographer Ansel Adams, who shared O'Keeffe's love for the desolate beauty of the Southwest, often joined her on sightseeing expeditions.

Admirers flocked to her shows, and her reputation as America's greatest woman painter remained unchallenged. In 1936 Elizabeth Arden, the cosmetics magnate, commissioned a massive O'Keeffe featuring white jimson blossoms for her swanky Manhattan exercise salon. Stieglitz negotiated the deal, and the painting sold for $10,000. O'Keeffe also created a delicate lily design for the renowned Steuben Glass Company, which engraved it on crystal bowls that sold for $500 each. In 1938, *Life* magazine featured a

photo essay on O'Keeffe and her work. Later that year, she was stunned when a garage mechanic recognized her when she arrived to pick up her car. "Why, I know you!" he exclaimed, and told her that he had cut a reproduction of one of her paintings out of *Life* and hung it up in his home. O'Keeffe's fame now transcended art circles; thousands of Americans were familiar with her work.

Stieglitz, even though he had suffered another heart attack and a bout with pneumonia, continued to worry about O'Keeffe's health and happiness during her summer trips. O'Keeffe, in turn, feared leaving him every spring, knowing full well that he was now a sick, old man and that each good-bye might be their last.

By this time, Stieglitz's friendship with Dorothy Norman had begun to wane, much to O'Keeffe's relief. No longer needed for An American Place's fund-raising efforts and tired of Stieglitz's stubborn lack of interest in the newest trends in art, Norman devoted her energies to her magazine, *Twice a Year: A Journal of Literature, the Arts, and Civil Liberties*. Stieglitz did include Norman in one draft of his will, but O'Keeffe saw to it that the will was changed.

In 1938, N. W. Ayer, the advertising agency for the Dole Pineapple Company, flew O'Keeffe to Hawaii on the condition that she make two paintings they might use on labels and in adver-

Stieglitz lectures art students on O'Keeffe's painting The Bone. *The energetic photographer worked to keep the reclusive painter's work before the public eye.*

tisements. She enjoyed the islands and executed a number of paintings of such brightly colored tropical flowers as hibiscus and lotus. During her visit, she wanted to stay at the pineapple fields with the native workers, but the Dole people turned down her request. Famous, white, female painters were not supposed to spend time with non-white, lower-class field workers.

Upon her return to New York three months later, O'Keeffe presented Dole with two paintings, one of a red ginger flower, the other of a papaya tree. The Dole representatives agreed that the pictures were striking, but what they really wanted was a painting of their major canning product, the pineapple. O'Keeffe responded that they had not specified her subject matter beforehand and had no right to dictate it now. N. W. Ayer's art director had a huge pineapple plant flown from Honolulu and delivered to her within 36 hours of their conversation. O'Keeffe grudgingly admitted that the plant was lovely and finally submitted a painting of a pineapple bud, which the Dole company used in various promotional pieces. If O'Keeffe had been allowed to stay with the pickers at the pineapple fields as she had requested, things would have gone more smoothly.

In the spring of 1939, after so many years of almost constant travel, O'Keeffe began to exhibit the symptoms that had heralded her breakdown six years earlier. She was moody and tired and had trouble eating and sleeping. Her headaches returned, and her doctor ordered her to remain in New York and rest.

O'Keeffe recovered much more quickly this time. Perhaps her spirits were buoyed at being named one of the 12 most outstanding women of the past 50 years by a committee of the New York World's Fair. By August she was able to travel to Lake George. She began painting again just a few months later.

In the summer of 1940, O'Keeffe returned to New Mexico and found strangers renting Rancho de los Burros. Feeling that the house rightfully belonged to her, she offered to buy the place outright from Arthur Pack. Pack agreed, and she reportedly paid him $6,000, the price of one of her major oil paintings.

It was probably the best investment O'Keeffe ever made. At last, she owned the house of her dreams.

This 1937 Adams photograph shows O'Keeffe flashing a grin at Orville Cox, a guide who led her and several others on an expedition through the Indian territory of New Mexico and Arizona.

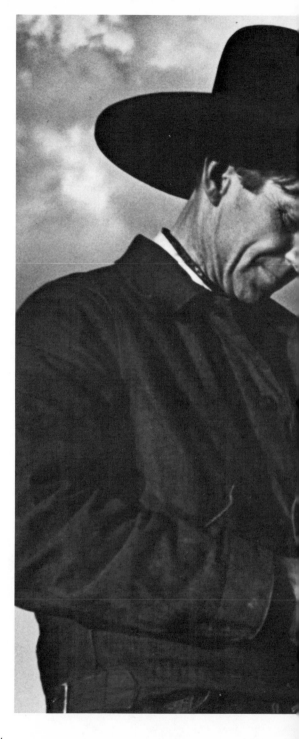

In the 1940s, O'Keeffe took her place as one of America's most celebrated painters. She received recognition from artists, scholars, and critics alike.

SEVEN

Life Without Stieglitz

As much as O'Keeffe loved her new home, Rancho de los Burros was not an easy place in which to live alone. The isolated house had no electricity and no phone to be used in case of emergency. She had to travel 80 miles to purchase food. Sudden storms sent dangerous flash floods raging down the nearby arroyos; rattlesnakes slithered into the house on cold nights to warm themselves by her fireplace. When they did, O'Keeffe could not bring herself to kill the reptiles. Instead, she calmly scooped them up with a shovel and deposited them outside.

O'Keeffe soon hired a young woman, Maria Chabot, to do the housekeeping. Freed from the drudgery of chores, O'Keeffe now spent 11 or 12 hours a day painting. She also roamed over the nearby hills on horseback, exploring places that could not be reached on foot or by car. And when the spirit moved them, she and her housekeeper would camp out in the desert.

On December 7, 1941, Japan bombed Pearl Harbor and America entered World War II. Life at the ranch became even more difficult when many of the ranch hands enlisted or were drafted into the army. Gas rationing began and civilians needed coupons to buy meat. However, remembering the resentment she had faced in Texas for her pacifist views during World War I, O'Keeffe was relieved to be left alone in her desert paradise, away from arguments about politics.

Much to her surprise, in 1942 both she and General Douglas MacArthur, the commander of U.S. forces in the

The USS Arizona *burns after the Japanese bombing of Pearl Harbor, which drew the United States into World War II. Wartime gas rationing restricted O'Keeffe's rambles through New Mexico.*

Pacific, received honorary doctorates from the University of Wisconsin. The fact that an artist and a general were both honored during wartime pleased O'Keeffe greatly. She attended the ceremony with her 87-year-old aunt Ollie.

She had had little contact with the surviving members of her family, but she was delighted to see her aunt, who had helped pay her art school fees when she was just starting out. Her father had died after falling from a roof in 1918. Francis, Jr., was an architect in Havana, Cuba, and her brother Alexius had died in 1930. Her sister Anita mar-

ried Robert Young, who became chairman of the board of the New York Central Railroad. Catherine and Ida both fancied themselves artists, and O'Keeffe greatly resented what she saw as their attempt to compete with her. Of all her siblings, she was closest to her sister Claudia, a teacher in Los Angeles, California.

O'Keeffe continued to return to New York each fall, in time for Stieglitz to arrange her annual exhibition. In 1942, she was approached by Daniel Catton Rich, curator of painting at the Art Institute of Chicago. He wanted to stage her first major retrospective. O'Keeffe agreed, and in January of 1943, she arrived in Chicago to oversee her first important show outside Stieglitz's An American Place.

The exhibit included paintings from every period of O'Keeffe's career, with 61 works dating from 1915 to 1941. O'Keeffe took pains to have the show presented exactly as she wanted it, demanding that the violet gallery walls be repainted white especially for her. When the show opened, audiences and most critics greeted it with enthusiasm and praise. As Marcia Winn, a reporter for the *Chicago Tribune* observed, "If you like her work, you love it. If you don't, you can't forget it."

The following summer, O'Keeffe began a series of paintings she called "The Bones and the Blue." During one of her rambles through the mountains of New Mexico, she found the sunbleached pelvic bone of a cow. When she looked at the sky through the oval hole in the center of the bone, she decided she had to paint the resulting scene. She used the pelvis in a number of paintings, capturing it in extreme closeups or setting it floating above the mountains with the moon shining through it. Some viewers thought the paintings represented O'Keeffe's views on war, a position supported by the essay she wrote for the catalogue that accompanied the first showing of the paintings. She wrote that the bones looked "wonderful against the Blue—

Stieglitz and O'Keeffe relax at his gallery, An American Place, in the 1940s. Mutual respect and shared creativity enriched their unconventional relationship until Stieglitz's death in 1946.

that Blue that will always be there as it is now after all man's destruction is finished."

In 1945, O'Keeffe bought a second house in Abiquiu. Tired of pumping her own water and living on canned food, she purchased an abandoned Spanish-style hacienda from the Catholic church. The soil was better there, and O'Keeffe could grow her own fruit and vegetables. She fixed up the house, furnishing it with simple wooden benches and creating an all-white studio with glass walls that enabled her to gaze down on the lovely Chama River

Valley. There, she found plenty of subject matter for her work, and set about recording her contemplations of nature in paintings such as *Spring Tree, No. 1* (see page 54).

By this time, Stieglitz's health had deteriorated significantly. Over 80 years old, he was very weak, able to walk only short distances. He spent much of his time at his gallery, napping on a cot in the back room, awaiting visitors who seldom came. His work had fallen out of fashion. The European painters who had emigrated to America during the war, such as Marc Chagall and Max Ernst, had little interest in the man who had introduced the world to the groundbreaking works of their predecessors. Whenever she was with her husband, O'Keeffe did her best to lift his sagging spirits. She encouraged acquaintances to visit Stieglitz, and spent much of her time caring for the man who, years before, had nurtured her career. In a letter to critic Henry McBride, she wrote, "Aside from my fondness for him personally I feel that he has been very important to something that has made my world for me—I like it that I can make him feel that I have hold of his hand to steady him as he goes on."

Paintings such as Black Place II *(1944) display O'Keeffe's unique boldness. The artist was annoyed when galleries and museums hung her paintings in corners so that they would not overpower the works of other artists.*

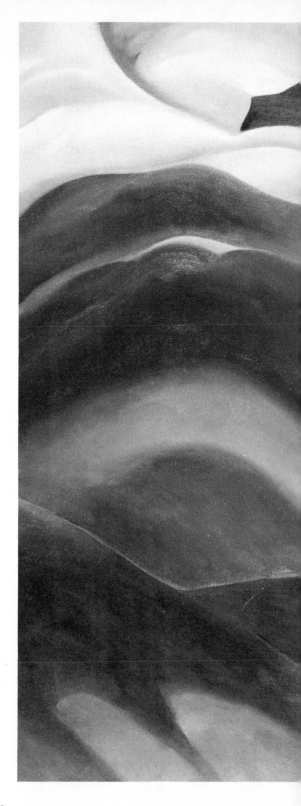

On July 6, 1946, while O'Keeffe was away in New Mexico, Stieglitz was stricken with chest pains while he was at An American Place. He seemed to recover, but a few days later he had a massive stroke and was admitted to the hospital.

More than 2,000 miles away, a telegraph office employee flagged down O'Keeffe's car with the news that Stieglitz was in critical condition at Doctors Hospital. Without stopping to pack or change her clothes, she drove to Albuquerque and caught the first plane to New York. When she arrived, her husband was in a coma.

Alfred Stieglitz died on Saturday, July 13, 1946. O'Keeffe purchased a simple pine coffin for her husband. She hated the pink satin lining and spent much of the night before the funeral carefully replacing it with plain white linen. After his body was cremated, she buried his ashes at the base of a pine tree on the banks of Lake George.

Only her closest friends knew how deeply Stieglitz's death had affected O'Keeffe. Outwardly, the artist remained calm and self-possessed, as if acknowledging the inevitability of losing her much-older husband. Privately, however, she confessed she missed Stieglitz greatly.

O'Keeffe became both the inheritor and executor of Stieglitz's estate. It was her responsibility to ensure that his art collection and personal effects be given to institutions that would properly care for them. It was a huge task: His estate included 850 works of modern art, hundreds of photographs, and 50,000 letters. Because Stieglitz had spent his most productive years in Manhattan, the bulk of his belongings went to New York's Metropolitan Museum. O'Keeffe's alma mater, the Art Institute of Chicago, received the second-largest lot. O'Keeffe spent three winters settling Stieglitz's estate. As a consequence, she accomplished little work of her own.

In 1949, O'Keeffe was elected to the National Institute of Arts and Letters by its members. She was especially proud of this honor because few women had previously won it. Only a tenth of the institute's members were women. Her election proved that members of the predominantly male art establishment had appreciated her work and understood the depth of her talent. It also meant that they had begun to recognize their female colleagues.

O'Keeffe tried to keep An American Place going, but without Stieglitz's vitality and enthusiasm, failure was inevitable. In the fall of 1950, O'Keeffe exhibited 31 of her own paintings there. It was An American Place's last show.

No longer needing to display her work annually to earn a living, O'Keeffe returned to New Mexico to live year round, staying at the ranch in summer and fall, in Abiquiu during winter and spring. Finding the cold temperatures and snowy landscape invigorating, she came to love New Mexico's winters.

She retreated into solitude, seeing friends only on holidays. She seemed to need no other people. She had her house, her mountains, her art. She was content to do paintings of her patio, rendering the door and windows on canvas again and again until she believed she had it right. (See for example, *In the Patio II*, page 55.)

If she shied from contact with other humans, O'Keeffe formed a rather unlikely attachment to a pair of Chinese chow pups a friend had given her. These fluffy, lionlike dogs possessed bright blue tongues and vicious tempers. O'Keeffe enjoyed their ferocity and their exotic appearance. She became absolutely devoted to the breed and even joined the International Chow Society.

After World War II, Arthur Pack and his family moved to Tucson, Arizona. Finding it difficult to manage the Ghost Ranch from such a great distance, he decided to donate the ranch to the United Presbyterian church.

When O'Keeffe, already disgruntled about the new roads and telephone lines appearing in her beloved wilderness, learned about the deal, she marched over to Pack's home. She had believed that Pack would give her the first chance to buy the ranch if he ever chose to sell it. Unmindful of the em-

O'Keeffe (back row, second from left) was one of 10 women—scientists, business leaders, and other notable achievers— chosen by the Women's National Press Club as 1945's "Makers and Promoters of Progress."

barrassed churchmen visiting to discuss the transaction, she said, "Now I suppose this beautiful place will be crawling with people and be completely spoiled. I never had any use for Presbyterians anyhow!" Nevertheless, Pack gave the ranch to the church.

O'Keeffe began traveling extensively in the 1950s, particularly during spring, when dust storms swept across the plains. She journeyed to Mexico and was entranced by the riot of color the peasant marketplaces created. In 1953, at the age of 66, she made her first trip to Europe, where she visited the most prestigious art museums on

O'Keeffe cradles a skull in her lap for this 1948 photograph showing her at home in the garden at Ghost Ranch.

the continent: the Louvre in France and the Prado in Spain. During this trip, a friend offered to introduce her to Pablo Picasso, by this time the world's most celebrated living artist. O'Keeffe refused. "I didn't care very much about looking at him, and I'm sure he didn't care about looking at me. I don't speak French, so we couldn't talk," she explained later. "My companion thought it was heretical, but if you can't talk, what's the point?"

In 1959, the 71-year-old O'Keeffe set off on a trip around the world, with stops in North America, Asia, the Middle East, and Europe. With her artist's eye, she sought out places and scenes that did not interest the average tourist. "I prefer the Far East to Europe," she noted wryly. "I like the dirty parts of the world." She also preferred the spare simplicity of Oriental art to the elaborate religious art she saw in Rome, which she termed "extraordinarily vulgar." She found the variety of people, architecture, and scenery she saw on her travels exhilarating, but no matter how far she roamed, her spiritual compass always pointed back to the Ghost Ranch and Abiquiu.

Having dropped out of the Manhattan art world after Stieglitz's death, O'Keeffe was soon forgotten by many of

O'Keeffe's popularity waned as the world turned its attention to abstract expressionism. Joan Mitchell created **King of Spades** *in 1956 using a technique called "action painting," in which the artist flings paint at the canvas.*

her former admirers. Painters known as "abstract expressionists" now commanded critics' attention with their bold spatters and wild brushstrokes of paint. If they thought of her at all, critics dismissed O'Keeffe, who had helped pioneer abstract art in America, as merely an historical footnote.

95

For O'Keeffe, shown here in her 94th year, the fascination with art and nature that had emerged in her childhood had always remained the prime force in her life.

EIGHT

Twilight in the Desert

In 1957, *Newsweek* magazine printed a story on O'Keeffe in its "Where Are They Now?" column. The artist who had so dazzled the art world for three decades was virtually unknown to a new generation of Americans.

Then Daniel Catton Rich, now director at Massachusetts's Worcester Art Museum, urged O'Keeffe to show her paintings at his museum. Trusting Rich because of the way he had handled her show at the Art Institute of Chicago, O'Keeffe agreed to let his museum house her first major exhibition since Stieglitz's death more than a decade earlier.

O'Keeffe spent much of 1960 preparing for the show: writing letters; selecting, framing, and shipping paintings; ensuring that the galleries were set up to her exact specifications. When the exhibition opened that autumn, it attracted the attention of many New York critics.

Although she had not been as prolific in recent years as she had been early in her career, the show included many new paintings, including some inspired by O'Keeffe's trip around the world. During her airplane journeys, she loved to look down at the glistening, colorful rivers that ran through many of the world's deserts. After sketching them on scraps of paper she kept in her purse, she transformed the sketches into drawings and paintings upon her return to New Mexico. Several of these vibrant oils had whimsical titles such as *It Was Yellow and Pink* and *It Was Red and Pink*. A later example of her work on this theme is *From the River, Light Blue*, painted in 1964 (see page 56).

These paintings baffled many viewers and critics. Some saw the rivers only as abstract shapes; others believed they might be tree branches. She was disappointed that many did not see her paintings as she did, but she was gratified by the response of at least one visitor to her exhibition. She wrote in her autobiography that "one day I saw a man looking around at my... showing. I heard him remark, 'They must be rivers seen from the air.' I was pleased that someone had seen what I saw and remembered it my way."

The Worcester show placed O'Keeffe back in the public eye. Although the response was mixed, most critics agreed that, as Daniel Rich put it, "at seventy-two O'Keeffe can still surprise herself.... she will continue to surprise all of us for quite some time." As time passed, his words seemed increasingly prophetic.

Intrigued by watching rivers from the air, O'Keeffe decided to take a closer look. She joined a group of friends on a 10-day, 185-mile raft trip down the upper part of the Colorado River in 1961. The 74-year-old artist demanded to pull her fair share of the load, allowing no one to help her with her equipment. At night, while camping on the sandbars, she arranged her sleeping bag to give her the most scenic view of the surrounding canyon walls.

Nature photographer Eliot Porter accompanied O'Keeffe on a number of subsequent river trips. He and O'Keeffe competed to see who could find the prettiest rocks. One day, Porter found a particularly beautiful smooth, black stone. O'Keeffe wanted it for her collection, but Porter refused, saying that he intended to give it to his wife.

When O'Keeffe visited the Porters at their home in Santa Fe the next Thanksgiving, they put the prized rock out on a coffee table for the sake of seeing what would happen. When she thought she was unobserved, O'Keeffe slipped the stone into her pocket. The Porters let her keep it. They understood that, one way or another, O'Keeffe usually got what she wanted.

In June 1965 O'Keeffe started work on the largest painting of her career. *Sky Above Clouds IV* measured a mammoth 24 feet by 8 feet. She worked on the painting in her unheated garage, the only space large enough to house the work. Racing to complete it before cold weather made it impossible to work, she painted daily from just after dawn until late evening. The finished painting depicted a sea of white oval clouds stretching off to a soft pink and blue horizon.

Sky Above Clouds IV was included in O'Keeffe's 1966 exhibition at the Amon Carter Museum of Western Art in Fort Worth, Texas. Parts of the show later traveled to the University of New Mexico in Albuquerque, where thousands of O'Keeffe's fellow New Mexicans flocked to see her first major exhibition in her adopted state.

More awards and recognition soon came O'Keeffe's way. She was elected

O'Keeffe's Sky Above Clouds IV *was inspired by a view from an airplane that she said "was so wonderful that I couldn't wait to be home to paint it."*

to the 50-member American Academy of Arts and Letters, the nation's highest honor society for men and women in the arts. *Life* magazine featured her in a lavishly illustrated cover story in 1968. In 1970, O'Keeffe opened her first show in New York since Stieglitz's death, a retrospective at the Whitney Museum. The show traveled to San Francisco and Chicago, earning O'Keeffe a whole new generation of admirers. Perhaps more importantly, O'Keeffe was pleased with her work. When she attended the exhibition with a friend, Blanche Matthias, she paused before a recent painting of the rock she had gotten from the Porters, *Black Rock with Blue*. According to Matthias, she paused before the painting, smiled to herself, and said, "It was the last thing I did, and the best."

The public was impressed not only by O'Keeffe's artistry but also by her appearance and personality. By now, the desert sun had browned her skin and etched deep lines in her face. Her white hair contrasted sharply with the black clothes she wore, and her dark eyebrows lent her face a severe expression when she was not smiling. She carried her thin body with a straight, assured bearing and spoke her mind without fear of contradiction.

One morning in 1971, O'Keeffe suddenly realized that her vision was blurred. Panicked and afraid she was losing her prized sharp eyesight, she consulted a number of specialists. She learned that she had lost her central

(Above and opposite) O'Keeffe assists the staff of the Amon Carter Museum in preparing her 1966 show. Insistent on the spare, dramatic exhibition spaces that showed her works to best advantage, she always supervised the installation of her shows.

vision and would be able to see only peripherally, out of the corners of her eyes. None of her doctors offered any remedy, saying that the affliction was common in the elderly. Frightened and depressed, O'Keeffe did little work during the next year.

One day in 1972, a dark-haired

young man stopped at her house to inquire about odd jobs. His name was Juan Hamilton, and he was a potter by trade. O'Keeffe was about to send him on his way, but something about his earnest, intelligent manner led her to offer him work wrapping up paintings for shipping. As time went by, O'Keeffe relied on Hamilton more and more to do small chores. Eventually she hired him as a full-time assistant.

O'Keeffe took an active interest in Hamilton's development as an artist, urging him to perfect his craft as a potter. He, in turn, encouraged her to try her hand at sculpture. She had

Potter Juan Hamilton encouraged O'Keeffe to try her hand at sculpture. She experimented briefly with clay, which enabled her to rely on her sense of touch rather than her failing eyesight.

worked with clay at school and never enjoyed it, but now that her eyesight was so poor, she began to consider working in the medium again. As she wrote in her autobiography, "As I watched him work with the clay I saw that he could make it speak. . . . I hadn't thought much about pottery but now I thought that maybe I could make a pot, too—maybe a beautiful pot—it could become another language for me."

But working exclusively with clay left her unsatisfied, and gradually, O'Keeffe's creative instinct forced her to take up her paintbrushes again. She claimed that her dimmed eyesight gave her a new way of looking at the world and inspired new paintings. She hired studio assistants to mix paints for her and do background brushwork. Several of the works she did during this period, such as *From a Day with Juan* and *Pink and Green Spring*, dis-

O'Keeffe prepares to work outdoors during the filming of a 1977 television documentary first aired on her 90th birthday.

played the same strong shapes and evocative colors that had marked her artwork from the beginning.

O'Keeffe never enjoyed writing about her work, preferring to let it stand on its own merits. In the middle seventies, however, she started work on an auto-biography. Although he had no experience in book publishing, Hamilton oversaw the production of the memoir, acting as O'Keeffe's eyes. *Georgia O'Keeffe*, published in the fall of 1976, featured more than 100 color-reproductions of O'Keeffe's paintings,

some never before displayed in public. It sold very well and received good reviews, although some readers were perplexed by O'Keeffe's unadorned, matter-of-fact writing style. Reviewer Sanford Schwartz commented that the book's tone was both "casual and re-gal," a description that seems equally appropriate for the author herself. Others were surprised at the small amount of space O'Keeffe devoted to her life with Stieglitz.

The American public grew increas-ingly fascinated with this elderly matriarch of modern art. On her 90th birthday in 1977, the Public Broadcasting System aired a television documentary about her life and career. The next year, New York's Metropolitan Museum of Art exhibited 51 of Stieglitz's famous photos of O'Keeffe. Popular magazines continued to print stories about her, and fans began to descend on Abiquiu, hoping to meet their idol in person.

No one could predict how O'Keeffe might greet an adoring visitor. If she was in a receptive mood, she might

Georgia O'Keeffe, Carmel Highlands, California, 1981. Photograph by Ansel Adams. Courtesy of the Trustees of The Ansel Adams Publishing Rights Trust. All Rights Reserved.

Georgia O'Keeffe's powerful individualism is apparent in this 1981 Ansel Adams photograph. The painter, who died in 1986, is remembered today as an independent spirit who quietly revolutionized the art world.

graciously invite a guest into her kitchen for a cup of tea and a brief chat. Or, as she herself reported, she might stop an intruder at the gate and say "Front side!" turn around and say "Back side!" and slam the gate shut with a resounding "Goodbye!"

In her old age, O'Keeffe tried to simplify her life and pare it down to the very basics, even in terms of human contact. She rarely saw her surviving sisters: Anita, Catherine, and Claudia. She broke off relationships with many of her friends, sometimes cruelly losing patience with their human frailties. O'Keeffe lost interest in seeing painter Dorothy Brett as Brett aged and grew increasingly eccentric. She also never forgave poet Spud Johnson after he missed an appointment she had made for him with the curator of the Stieglitz archive at Yale.

People wondered if she was lonely in her house in the desert, but O'Keeffe claimed to be content with her reclusive life. She liked talking and joking with Juan Hamilton and enjoyed the company of her chow dogs. She employed housekeepers and assistants to look after her, but she said that other people usually just bothered her.

O'Keeffe liked to say that she would live to be 100. When she passed her 90th birthday, she upped the figure to 125. She would admit no fear of death. She once said, "When I think of death, I only regret that I will not be able to see this beautiful country anymore, unless the Indians are right and my spirit will walk here after I'm gone."

O'Keeffe did not see her 125th birthday, but she very nearly fulfilled her earlier prediction. She died on March 6, 1986, at the age of 98.

In the course of a long, prolific career, Georgia O'Keeffe helped to define modern American art. A woman who knew precisely what she wanted from life and was not afraid to reach out and grab it, she made her mark in a field previously believed to be the exclusive domain of men. Unmindful of trends and fashions, she remained true to her own inner vision, which she eloquently expressed time and time again on canvas. No one who has seen her work will ever look at a flower, a skyscraper, or a desert landscape without being reminded of the extraordinary woman who depicted them with the compelling, almost mystical, language that was her art.

FURTHER READING

Castro, Jan Garden. *The Art & Life of Georgia O'Keeffe.* New York: Crown, 1985.

Calloway, Nicholas, ed. *One Hundred Flowers.* New York: Knopf, 1987.

Cowart, Jack, Juan Hamilton, and Sarah Greenough, eds. *Georgia O'Keeffe.* Boston: Little Brown & Company in association with the National Gallery of Art and the New York Graphic Society, 1987.

Goodrich, Lloyd, and Doris Bry. *Georgia O'Keeffe.* Exhibition catalog for Whitney Museum of American Art. New York: Praeger Publishers, 1970.

Hoffman, Katherine. *An Enduring Spirit: The Art of Georgia O'Keeffe.* Metuchen, NJ: Scarecrow Press, 1984.

Lisle, Laurie. *Portrait of an Artist: A Biography of Georgia O'Keeffe.* New York: Washington Square Press, 1981.

O'Keeffe, Georgia. *Georgia O'Keeffe.* New York: Viking, 1976.

————. *Georgia O'Keeffe: Works on Paper.* Exhibition catalog for Museum of Fine Arts, Santa Fe. Santa Fe, NM: Museum of New Mexico Press, 1984.

Webb, Todd. *Georgia O'Keeffe: The Artist's Landscape.* Pasadena, CA: Twelvetree Press, 1984.

CHRONOLOGY

Nov. 15, 1887	Georgia O'Keeffe born in Sun Prairie, Wisconsin
1905–06	Studies at the Art Institute of Chicago
1907–08	Attends the Art Students League in New York
1908–10	Works as a free-lance illustrator in Chicago
1912–14	Teaches art in Amarillo, Texas
1914–15	Studies art at Columbia University Teachers College
1916	Alfred Stieglitz holds first exhibition of O'Keeffe's work
1916–18	O'Keeffe teaches art at West Texas State Normal College
June 1918	Moves to New York; begins painting full-time
1923	Opens a successful one-woman show at the Anderson Galleries
Dec. 11, 1924	Marries Stieglitz
1928	Sells a series of calla lily panels for $25,000
April 1929	Visits New Mexico for the first time
Feb. 1933	Is hospitalized following a nervous breakdown
Feb. 1938	Travels and paints in Hawaii as a guest of the Dole Pineapple Company
1943	The Art Institute of Chicago stages O'Keeffe's first major retrospective
July 13, 1946	Stieglitz dies
1946–49	O'Keeffe oversees the distribution of Stieglitz's art collection
1949	Elected to the National Institute of Arts and Letters
1950	Moves to New Mexico permanently
1959	Travels to Asia, the Middle East, and Europe
Oct. 1960	Holds first large exhibition since 1946, at Worcester Art Museum
1965	Paints *Sky Above Clouds IV*, the largest painting of her career
1970	Opens a major retrospective of her work at New York's Whitney Museum
1976	Publishes her autobiography, *Georgia O'Keeffe*
March 6, 1986	Dies at age 98

INDEX

INDEX

PICTURE CREDITS

Michael Berry is a promotional copywriter for two major daily newspapers in San Francisco. He has contributed to *Saturday Review* and *Air & Space* and reviews science fiction for the *San Francisco Chronicle*. A native of Portsmouth, New Hampshire, he now lives in Berkeley, California.

❖   ❖   ❖

Matina S. Horner is president of Radcliffe College and associate professor of psychology and social relations at Harvard University. She is best known for her studies of women's motivation, achievement, and personality development. Dr. Horner serves on several national boards and advisory councils, including those of the National Science Foundation, Time Inc., and the Women's Research and Education Institute. She earned her B.A. from Bryn Mawr College and Ph.D. from the University of Michigan, and holds honorary degrees from many colleges and universities, including Mount Holyoke, Smith, Tufts, and the University of Pennsylvania.